Victorian Domestic Architectural Plans and Details

—◆·◆—

Victorian Domestic Architectural Plans and Details

734 Scale Drawings of Doorways,
Windows, Staircases, Moldings, Cornices and Other Elements

WILLIAM T. COMSTOCK

DOVER PUBLICATIONS, INC., NEW YORK

IMPORTANT NOTE

In this reprint edition, all plates have been reduced by 12 percent. Readers should bear this in mind when dealing with the scales given on the plates.

Published in Canada by General Publishing Company, Ltd.,
30 Lesmill Road, Don Mills, Toronto, Ontario.
Published in the United Kingdom by Constable and Company, Ltd.

This Dover edition, first published in 1987, is a slightly revised republication of the work originally published by William T. Comstock (Successor to Bicknell & Comstock), Architectural Publisher, New York, in 1881 under the title *Modern Architectural Designs and Details: Containing Eighty Finely Lithographed Plates, Showing New and Original Designs in the Queen Anne, Eastlake, Elizabethan, and Other Modernized Styles, Giving Perspective Views, Floor and Framing Plans, Elevations, Sections, and a great Variety of miscellaneous Exterior and Interior Details of Dwellings of Moderate Cost. Also, a number of Designs of Low Priced Cottages in the Various Popular Styles, Adapted to the Requirements of Seaside and Summer Resorts, and Suburban and Country Places. Also, Several Designs for Modern Store and Office Fronts, Counters, Shelvings, etc., etc., Comprising Original Drawings by a Number of Prominent Architects of Different Localities, Prepared Expressly for this Work.* The German translations of the Preface and the Table of Contents, as well as the twelve pages of advertisements that appeared at the back of the original edition, have been omitted from the present edition. The plates, unbacked in the original edition, are here reprinted on both the front and back sides of the pages.

Manufactured in the United States of America
Dover Publications, Inc., 31 East 2nd Street, Mineola, N.Y. 11501

Library of Congress Cataloging-in-Publication Data

Victorian domestic architectural plans and details.

Rev. ed. of: Modern architectural designs and details. c1881.
1. Architecture, Victorian—United States—Designs and plans.
2. Architecture, Domestic—United States—Designs and plans.
3. Architecture, Modern—19th century—United States—Designs and plans.
4. Architecture—Details.
I. Comstock, William T. Modern architectural designs and details.
II. Title.
NA7207.V53   1987   728'.022'2   87-9224
ISBN 0-486-25442-9 (pbk.)

PREFACE

IN offering this work to the public, it may not be out of place to refer to the purpose we (Mr. Bicknell, my former partner, and myself) had in view in its preparation. Our intention primarily was to make it a work of Architectural details, suited to the present styles. Some few years have elapsed since Mr. Bicknell brought out his "Detail Cottage and Constructive Architecture," his last work on details, and during that time a great change has taken place in the style of Architecture. The French, then largely in vogue, has been supplanted by our present modified Gothic, which appears as "Queen Anne," "Elizabethan," "Jacobean," or "Colonial," and is a revival of the old Gothic, as it appeared during the periods referred to under these respective names. The present styles, while bearing many characteristics of their prototypes, do not adhere strictly to any of them. Thus, in what is known as the Queen Anne (of the present day) is frequently introduced classic features, and the same is true of the other styles. So radical a change made it seem necessary to give a large number of complete designs for houses, as well as details of detached portions, which we have accordingly done, our purpose being to furnish good examples of complete buildings, as well as practical details.

In gathering the material for this work we have endeavored to select from the best sources, and have enlisted the services of several men prominent in their profession, with the intent of giving the greatest variety possible in the compass of such a work.

As will be observed by referring to the different designs, we have studied to make this work one of practical utility.

All plans, elevations and Details are drawn to scale. The elevations have been worked out with care, so that they may be clearly understood without further explanation than is furnished by the drawings. In some cases we have shown the construction by full framing plans. Details are given in great variety and abundance, amounting to nearly 700 in all, and drawn to a large scale. They will be found to cover almost every question that can arise in detailing a modern dwelling.

We have avoided giving many costly designs, but think the large number of low-priced, yet picturesque, designs of good character given in this work has not been exceeded in any former Architectural publication.

Stores and their details have been given suitable, though limited, attention.

In closing, it may not be out of place to refer to the manner in which the work has been executed. The entire set of plates has been engraved on stone. We have adopted this method in this publication, although at a large expense, in preference to the cheaper photo-lithographic processes, in order that every line may be clearly defined and the scale accurately preserved, and think the appreciation of practical men will be ample recompense for the extra outlay.

WILLIAM T. COMSTOCK

NEW YORK, July 1st, 1881.

CONTENTS

COUNTRY HOUSES AND COTTAGES.

STORES.

DETAILS OF DESIGNS AND MISCELLANEOUS DETAILS.

Victorian Domestic Architectural Plans and Details

Plate 1

Perspective View.

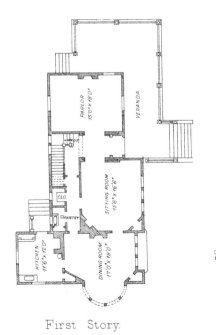

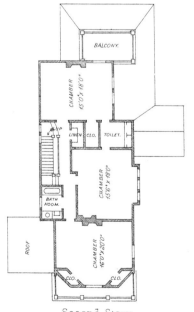

First Story.

Second Story.

House at Summit,
N. J.
LAMB & WHEELER, ARCHᵀˢ

SCALE

0 1 2 3 4 5   10   15   20   25   30   35   40.

Plate 2

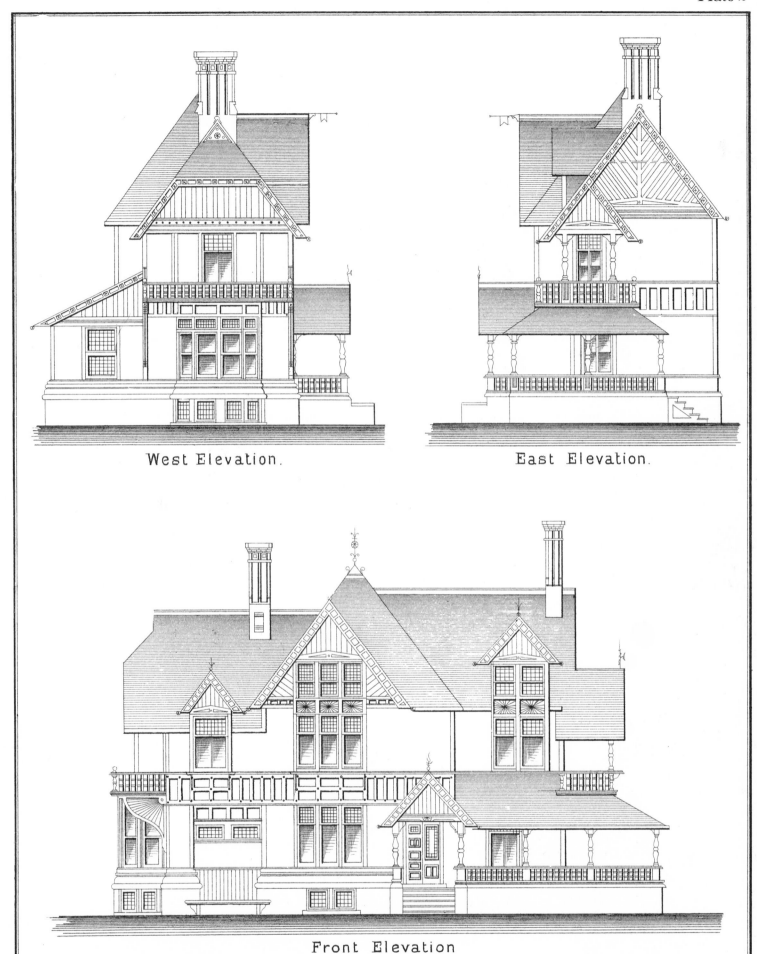

West Elevation.

East Elevation.

Front Elevation

SCALE 3/32" = 1 FOOT.

Lamb & Wheeler, Arch^ts
145 Broadway, N.Y.

Plate 3

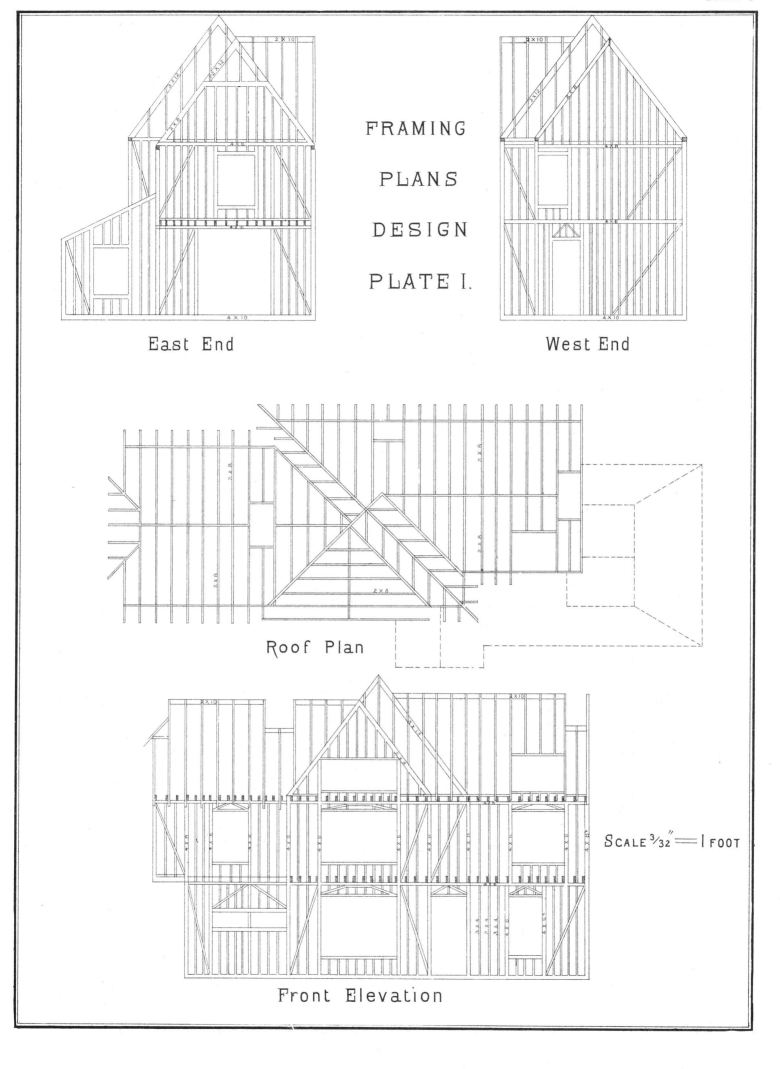

East End

West End

FRAMING

PLANS

DESIGN

PLATE I.

Roof Plan

Front Elevation

SCALE 3/32" = 1 FOOT

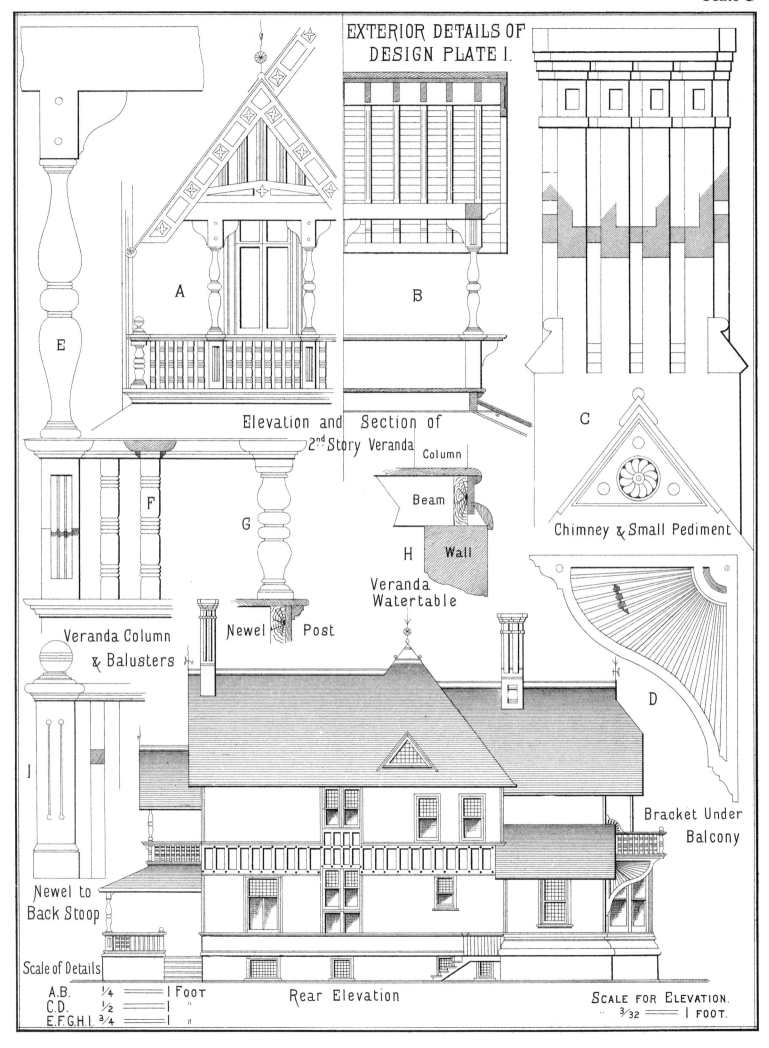

Plate 4

EXTERIOR DETAILS OF
DESIGN PLATE I.

A

B

E

Elevation and Section of
2nd Story Veranda

Column

Beam

F

G

H

Wall

Veranda
Watertable

C

Chimney & Small Pediment

D

Veranda Column
& Balusters

Newel Post

Bracket Under
Balcony

I

Newel to
Back Stoop

Rear Elevation

Scale of Details

A.B.   ¼   1 Foot
C.D.   ½   1 "
E.F.G.H.I. ¾   1 "

SCALE FOR ELEVATION.
3/32   1 FOOT.

Plate 5

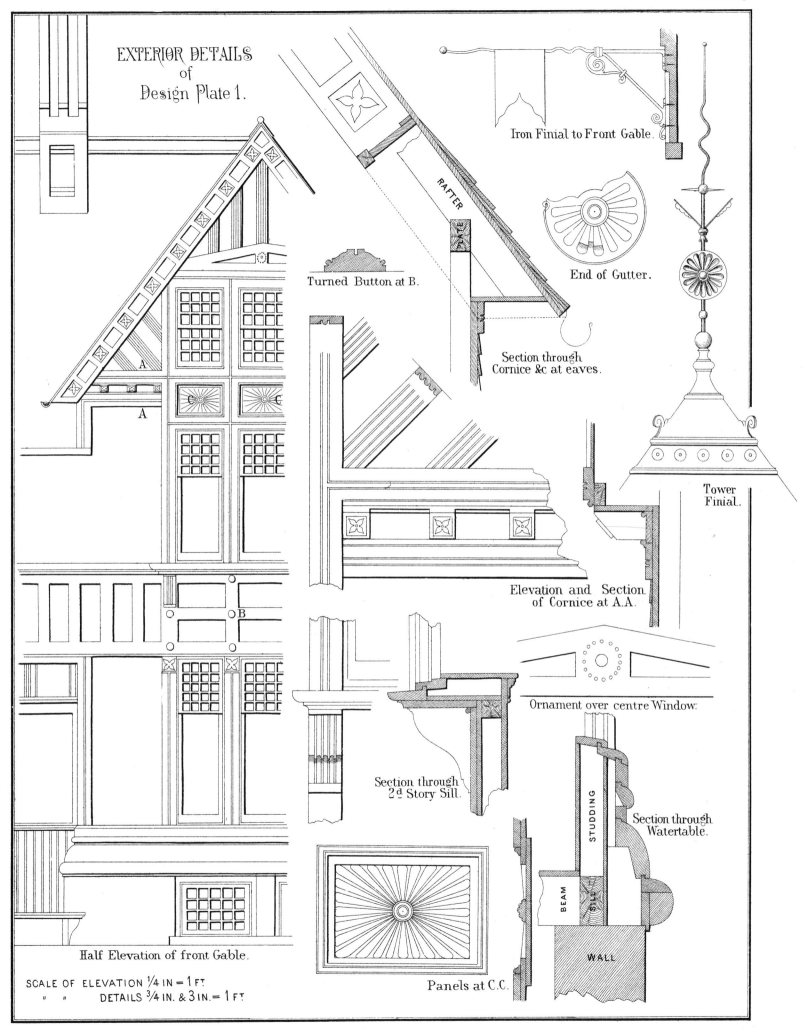

EXTERIOR DETAILS
of
Design Plate 1.

Turned Button at B.

Iron Finial to Front Gable.

RAFTER

End of Gutter.

Section through
Cornice &c at eaves.

Tower
Finial.

A

C C

A

B

Elevation and Section
of Cornice at A.A.

Ornament over centre Window.

Section through
2ᵈ Story Sill.

STUDDING

Section through
Watertable.

BEAM

SILL

WALL

Half Elevation of front Gable.

Panels at C.C.

SCALE OF ELEVATION ¼ IN = 1 FT.
"   "   DETAILS ¾ IN. & 3 IN. = 1 FT.

Plate 6

INTERIOR DETAILS OF DESIGN PLATE I.

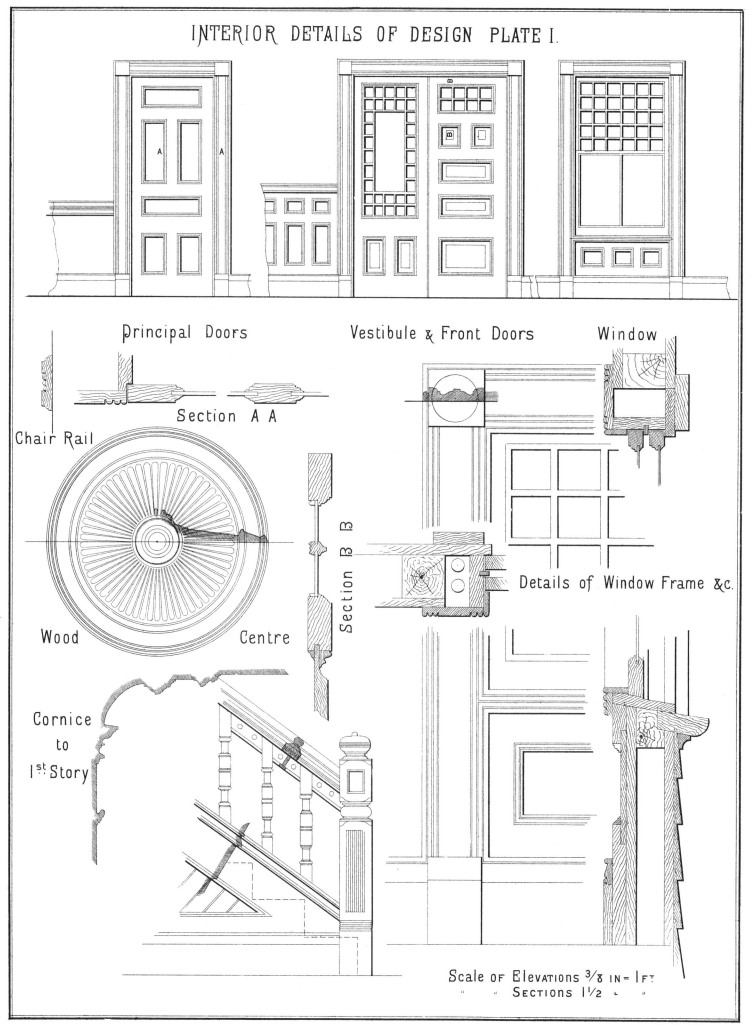

Principal Doors

Vestibule & Front Doors

Window

Chair Rail

Section A A

Section B B

Wood   Centre

Details of Window Frame &c.

Cornice
to
1st Story

Scale of Elevations 3/8 in = 1 ft.
"   " Sections 1½ "   "

Plate 7

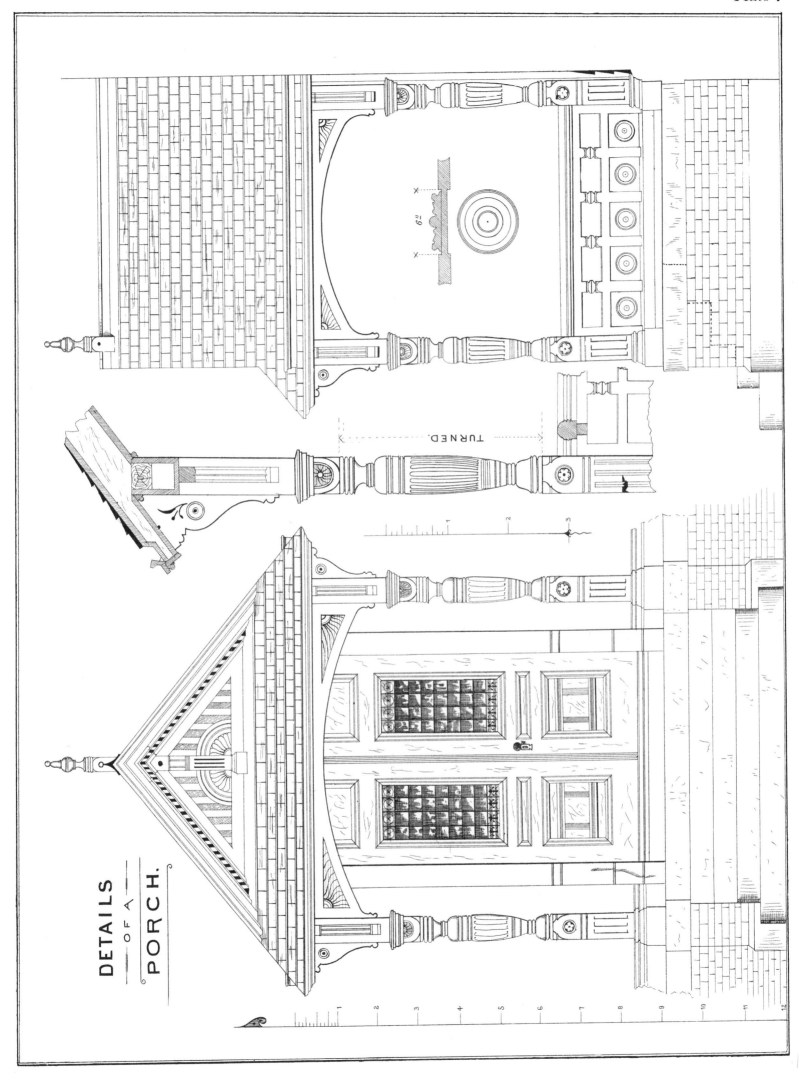

DETAILS OF A PORCH.

Plate 8

Piazzas.

A.

B.

C.

DESIGNS SCALE ½ IN−1 FT.
SECTIONS A.B.C. ¾ , , ,

Plate 9

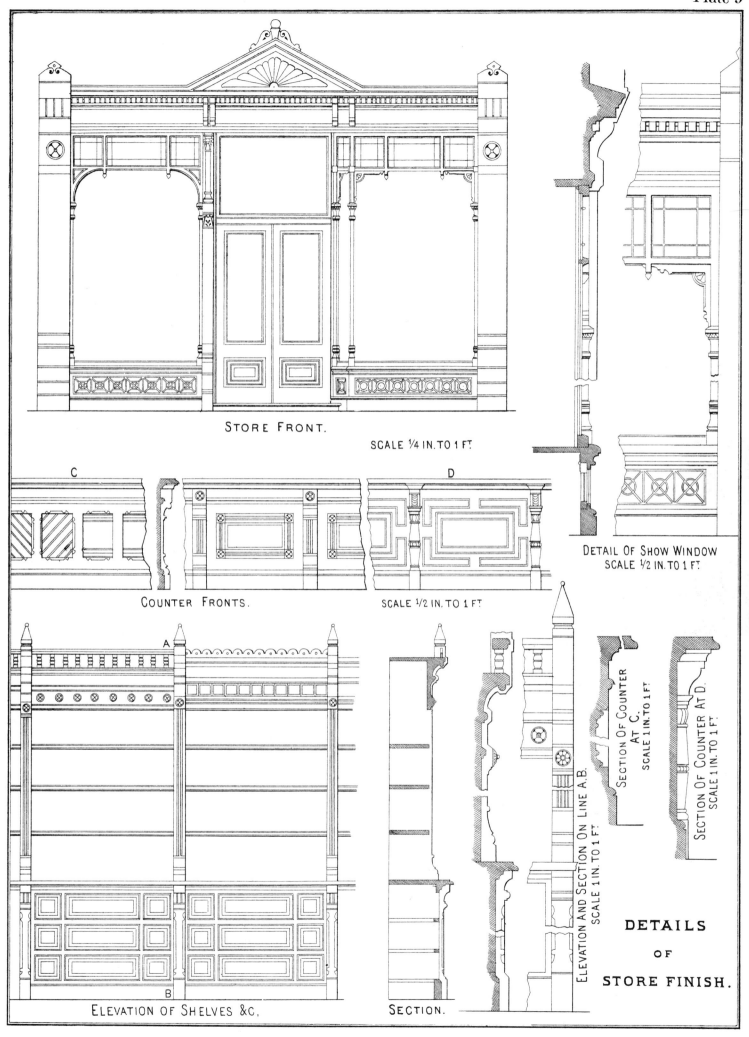

STORE FRONT.

SCALE ¼ IN. TO 1 FT.

DETAIL OF SHOW WINDOW
SCALE ½ IN. TO 1 FT.

C

D

COUNTER FRONTS.

SCALE ½ IN. TO 1 FT.

A

B

ELEVATION OF SHELVES &C.

SECTION.

ELEVATION AND SECTION ON LINE A.B.
SCALE 1 IN. TO 1 FT.

SECTION OF COUNTER AT C.
SCALE 1 IN. TO 1 FT.

SECTION OF COUNTER AT D.
SCALE 1 IN. TO 1 FT.

DETAILS
OF
STORE FINISH.

Plate 10

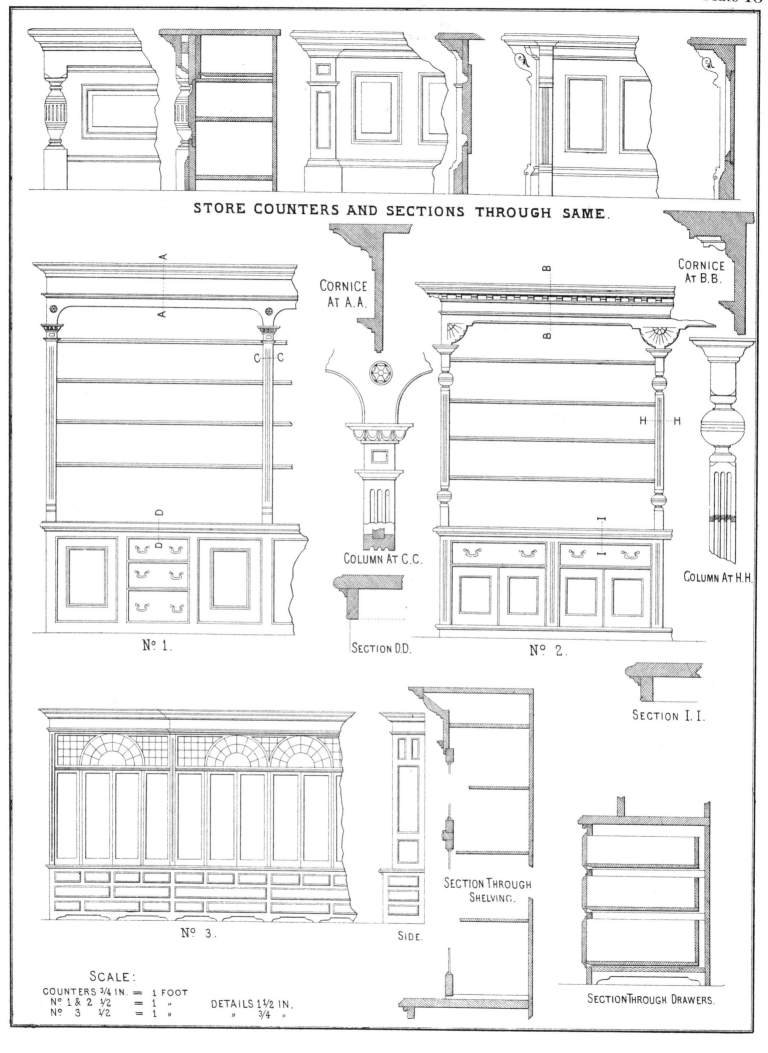

STORE COUNTERS AND SECTIONS THROUGH SAME.

CORNICE AT A.A.

CORNICE AT B.B.

COLUMN AT C.C.

COLUMN AT H.H.

SECTION D.D.

Nº 1.

Nº 2.

SECTION I.I.

Nº 3.

SIDE.

SECTION THROUGH SHELVING.

SECTION THROUGH DRAWERS.

SCALE:
COUNTERS ¾ IN. = 1 FOOT
Nº 1 & 2 ½ = 1 "   DETAILS 1½ IN.
Nº 3 ½ = 1 "   " ¾ "

Plate 15

BALCONIES.

FIG. 1.

FIG. 2.

FIG. 3.

FIG. 2. D

FIG. 4.

ELEVATIONS
SCALE ⅜ IN. = 1 FT

DETAILS
SCALE ¾ IN = 1 FT

Plate 16

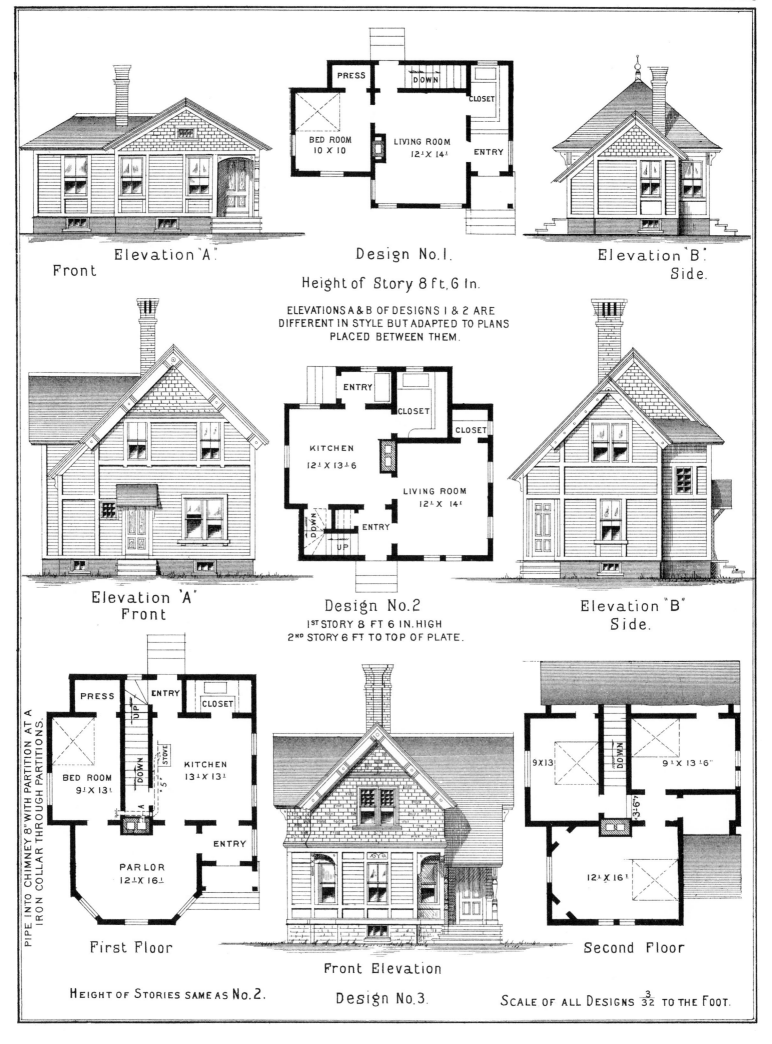

Elevation "A".
Front

Design No. 1.

Height of Story 8 ft. 6 In.

Elevation "B".
Side.

PRESS

DOWN

CLOSET

BED ROOM
10 X 10

LIVING ROOM
12¹ X 14¹

ENTRY

ELEVATIONS A & B OF DESIGNS 1 & 2 ARE
DIFFERENT IN STYLE BUT ADAPTED TO PLANS
PLACED BETWEEN THEM.

Elevation 'A'
Front

Design No. 2
1ST STORY 8 FT 6 IN. HIGH
2ND STORY 6 FT TO TOP OF PLATE.

Elevation "B"
Side.

ENTRY

CLOSET

CLOSET

KITCHEN
12¹ X 13¹ 6

LIVING ROOM
12¹ X 14¹

DOWN

UP

ENTRY

PIPE INTO CHIMNEY 8" WITH PARTITION AT A
IRON COLLAR THROUGH PARTITIONS.

PRESS

ENTRY

CLOSET

UP

DOWN

STOVE

5'

BED ROOM
9¹ X 13¹

KITCHEN
13¹ X 13¹

ENTRY

PARLOR
12¹ X 16¹

First Floor

HEIGHT OF STORIES SAME AS NO. 2.

Front Elevation

Design No. 3.

9 X 13

DOWN

9¹ X 13¹ 6"

3'-6"

12¹ X 16¹

Second Floor

SCALE OF ALL DESIGNS ³⁄₃₂ TO THE FOOT.

Plate 17

Low Priced Queen Anne Cottages.

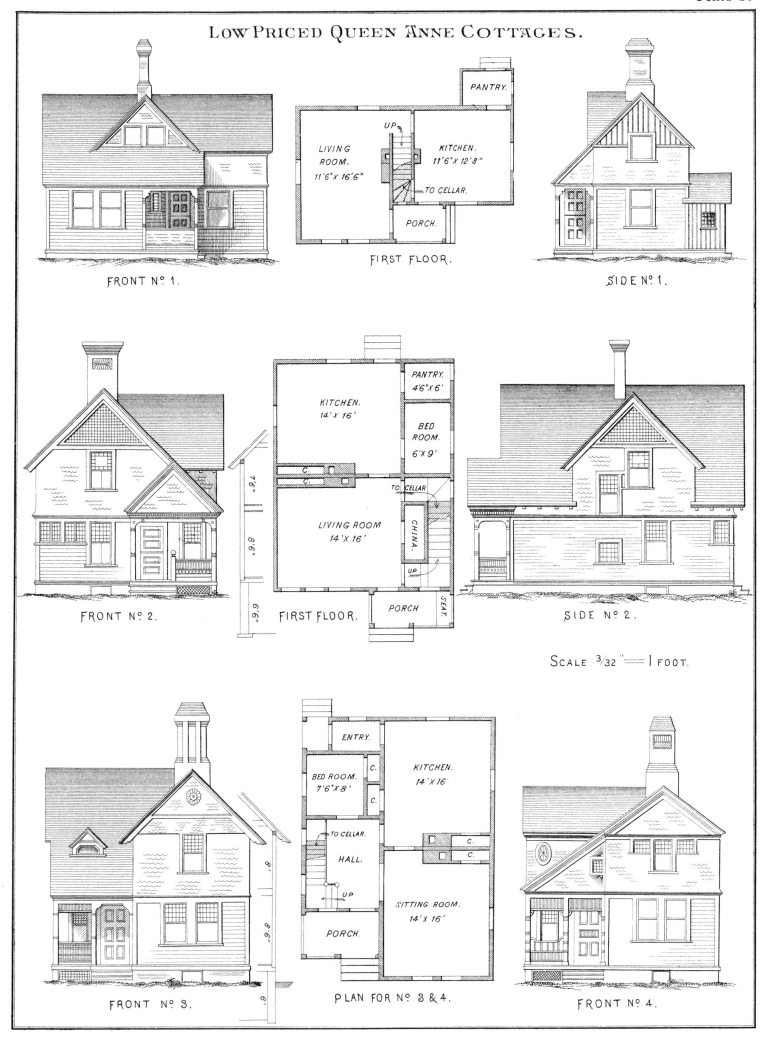

FRONT N° 1.

FIRST FLOOR.

SIDE N° 1.

PANTRY.

LIVING ROOM. 11'6" X 16'6"

UP

KITCHEN. 11'6" X 12'8"

TO CELLAR.

PORCH.

FRONT N° 2.

FIRST FLOOR.

SIDE N° 2.

KITCHEN. 14' X 16'

PANTRY. 4'6" X 6'

BED ROOM. 6' X 9'

C. C.

TO CELLAR

CHINA.

LIVING ROOM 14' X 16'

UP

PORCH

SEAT.

7'6"

8'6"

9'6"

Scale 3/32" = 1 Foot.

FRONT N° 3.

PLAN FOR N° 3 & 4.

FRONT N° 4.

ENTRY.

BED ROOM 7'6" X 8'

C. C.

KITCHEN. 14' X 16'

TO CELLAR.

HALL.

UP

C. C.

SITTING ROOM. 14' X 16'

PORCH.

8'6"

8'6"

9'6"

Plate 20

FRONT ELEVATION.

SCALE 1/8 IN = 1 FT

WEST ELEVATION.　　　SCALE 1/16 IN = 1 FT　　　EAST ELEVATION.

Elevations.

Design Plate 19.

Plate 21

FRAMING PLANS DESIGN PLATE 19.

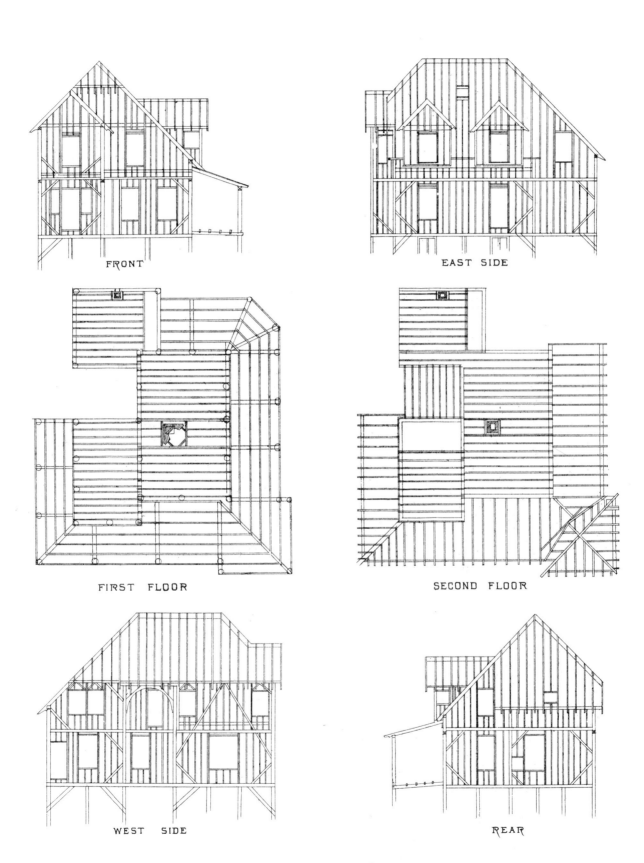

FRONT

EAST SIDE

FIRST FLOOR

SECOND FLOOR

WEST SIDE

REAR

Scale ¹⁄₁₆" = 1 ft.

Plate 22

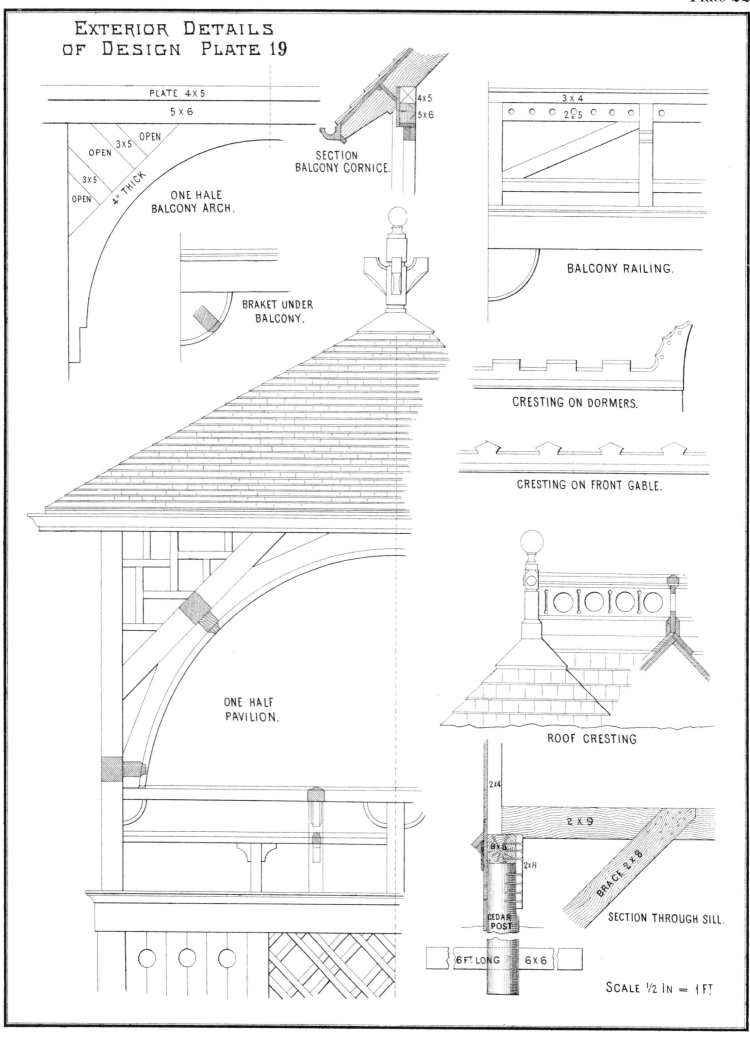

EXTERIOR DETAILS
OF DESIGN PLATE 19

PLATE 4 X 5
5 X 6

OPEN
3X5 OPEN
OPEN 3X5
3X5 4" THICK
OPEN

ONE HALE
BALCONY ARCH.

SECTION
BALCONY CORNICE.

4X5
5X6

3 X 4
2 X 5

BALCONY RAILING.

BRAKET UNDER
BALCONY.

CRESTING ON DORMERS.

CRESTING ON FRONT GABLE.

ONE HALF
PAVILION.

ROOF CRESTING

2X4
2 X 9
3X8
2X8
BRACE 2 X 8
CEDAR
POST

SECTION THROUGH SILL.

6 FT. LONG   6X6

SCALE ½ IN = 1 FT.

Plate 23

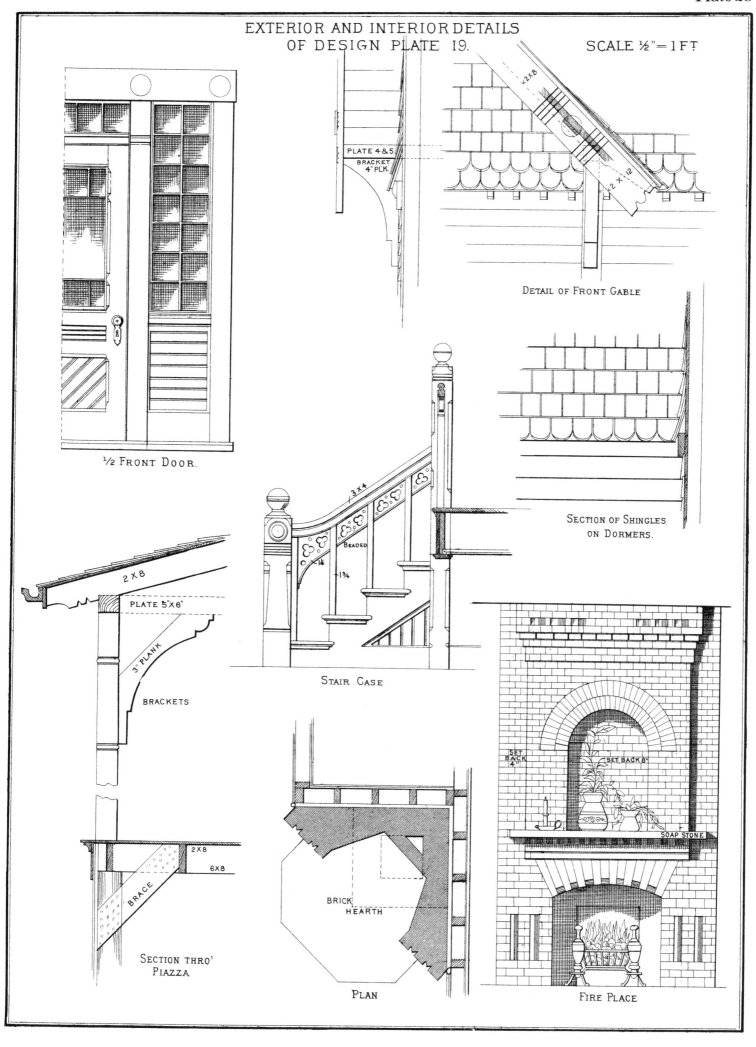

EXTERIOR AND INTERIOR DETAILS
OF DESIGN PLATE 19.

SCALE ½"= 1 FT.

½ FRONT DOOR.

DETAIL OF FRONT GABLE

SECTION OF SHINGLES
ON DORMERS.

STAIR CASE

BRACKETS

SECTION THRO'
PIAZZA

PLAN

FIRE PLACE

Plate 24

WINDOW SASH QUEEN ANNE STYLE.

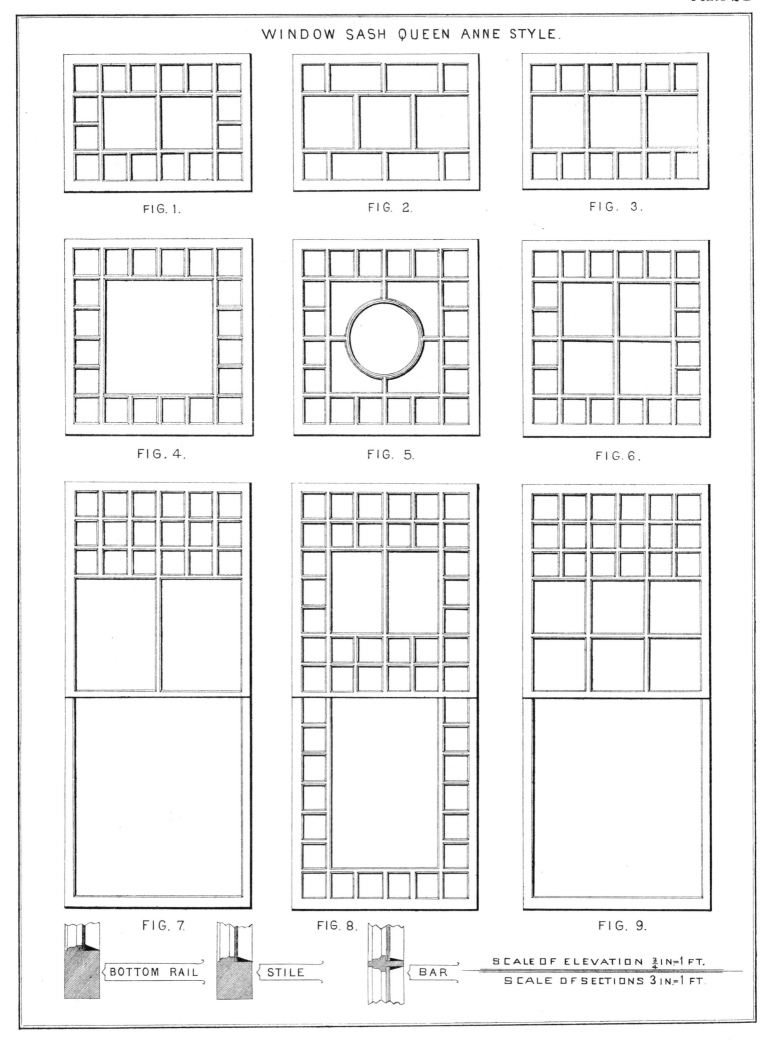

FIG. 1.   FIG. 2.   FIG. 3.

FIG. 4.   FIG. 5.   FIG. 6.

FIG. 7.   FIG. 8.   FIG. 9.

BOTTOM RAIL   STILE   BAR

SCALE OF ELEVATION ¾ IN=1 FT.
SCALE OF SECTIONS 3 IN=1 FT.

Plate 25

STORE FRONTS AND DETAILS.

SIDE

FRONT ELEVATION.

MAIN CORNICE

VERANDA
AND
BALCONY.

FRONT ELEVATION.

STORE
24 X 40

DINING
ROOM
10'6" X 13'0"

KITCHEN
12 X 12'6"

BED ROOM
8 X 12'

BED ROOM
8 X 9'6"

BED ROOM
7'6" X 6

PARLOR
12'6" X 15

BED ROOM
8 X 12'8

SCALES

PLANS   1/16" SCALE
ELEVATIONS 1/8 "
DETAILS   3/4 "

FIRST STORY.

SECOND STORY.

MAIN CORNICE

Plate 26

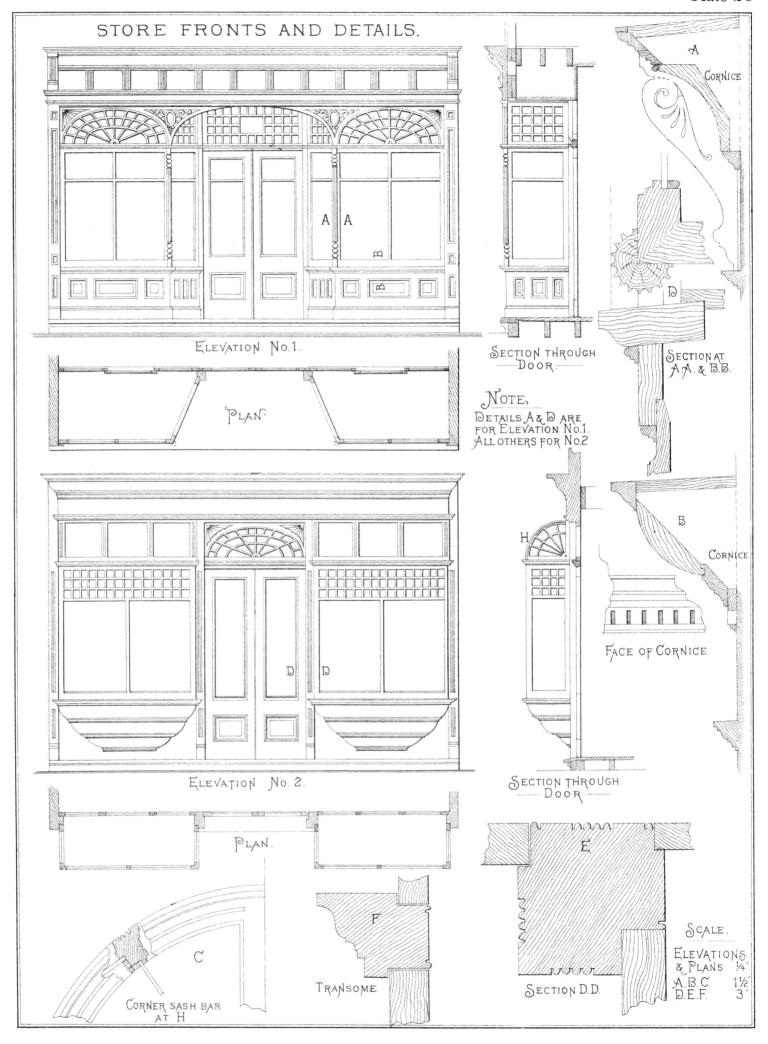

STORE FRONTS AND DETAILS.

ELEVATION No.1.

PLAN

ELEVATION No. 2.

PLAN.

CORNER SASH BAR
AT H

C

SECTION THROUGH
DOOR.

NOTE.
DETAILS A & D ARE
FOR ELEVATION No.1.
ALL OTHERS FOR No.2

SECTION THROUGH
DOOR

TRANSOME

A
CORNICE

SECTION AT
A.A. & B.B.

B

CORNICE

FACE OF CORNICE

E

SECTION D.D.

SCALE.
ELEVATIONS
& PLANS   ¼"
A.B.C.   1½"
D.E.F.   3"

F

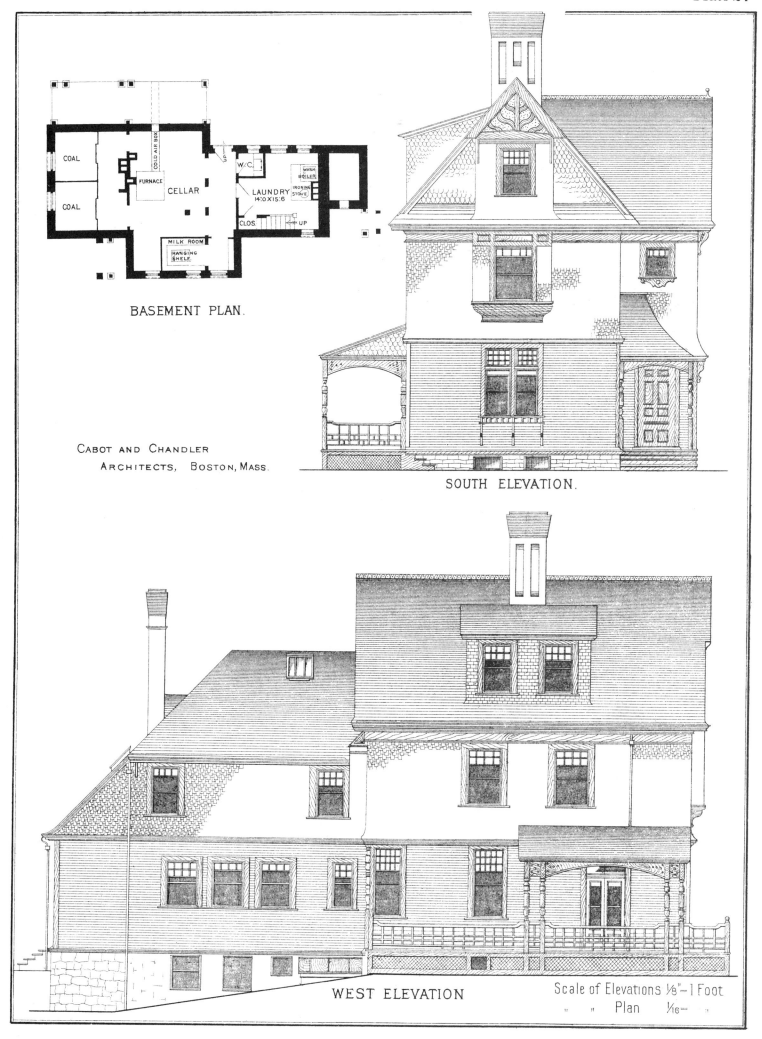

Plate 27

BASEMENT PLAN.

COAL
COAL
FURNACE
CELLAR
COLD AIR BOX
W.C.
WASH BOILER
IRONING STOVE
LAUNDRY 14:0 X15:6
CLOS.
MILK ROOM
HANGING SHELF

CABOT AND CHANDLER
ARCHITECTS, BOSTON, MASS.

SOUTH ELEVATION.

WEST ELEVATION

Scale of Elevations ⅛"–1 Foot
Plan ¹⁄₁₆=

Plate 28

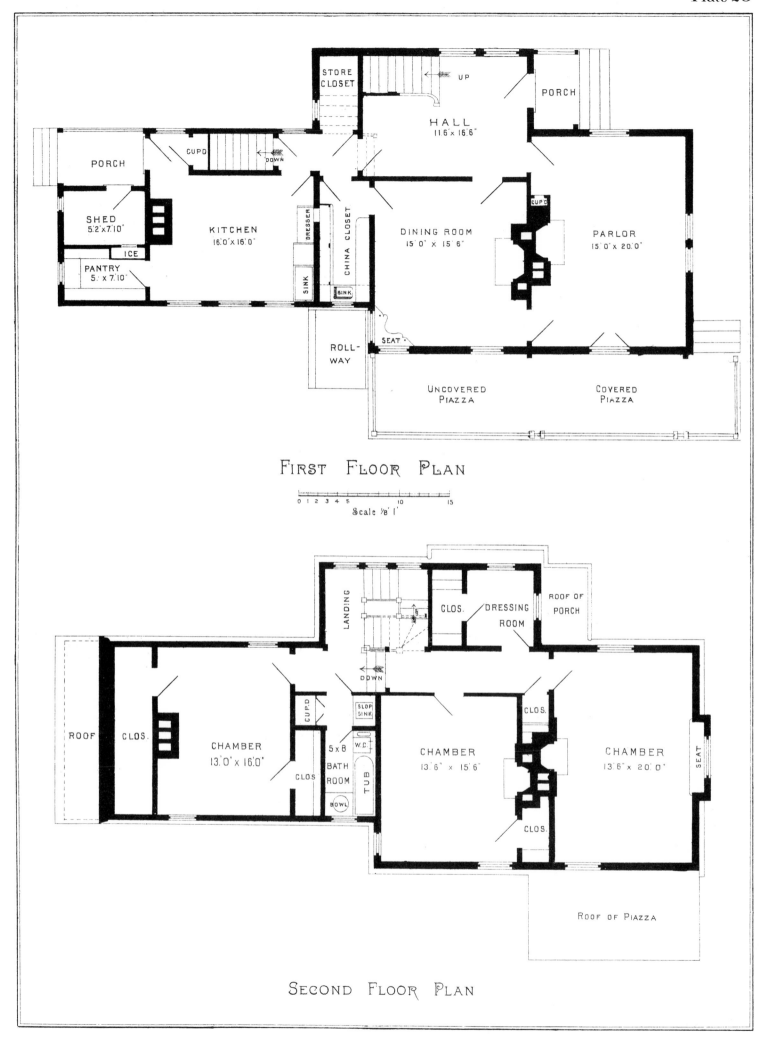

FIRST FLOOR PLAN

0 1 2 3 4 5   10   15
Scale ⅛' 1'

SECOND FLOOR PLAN

Plate 29

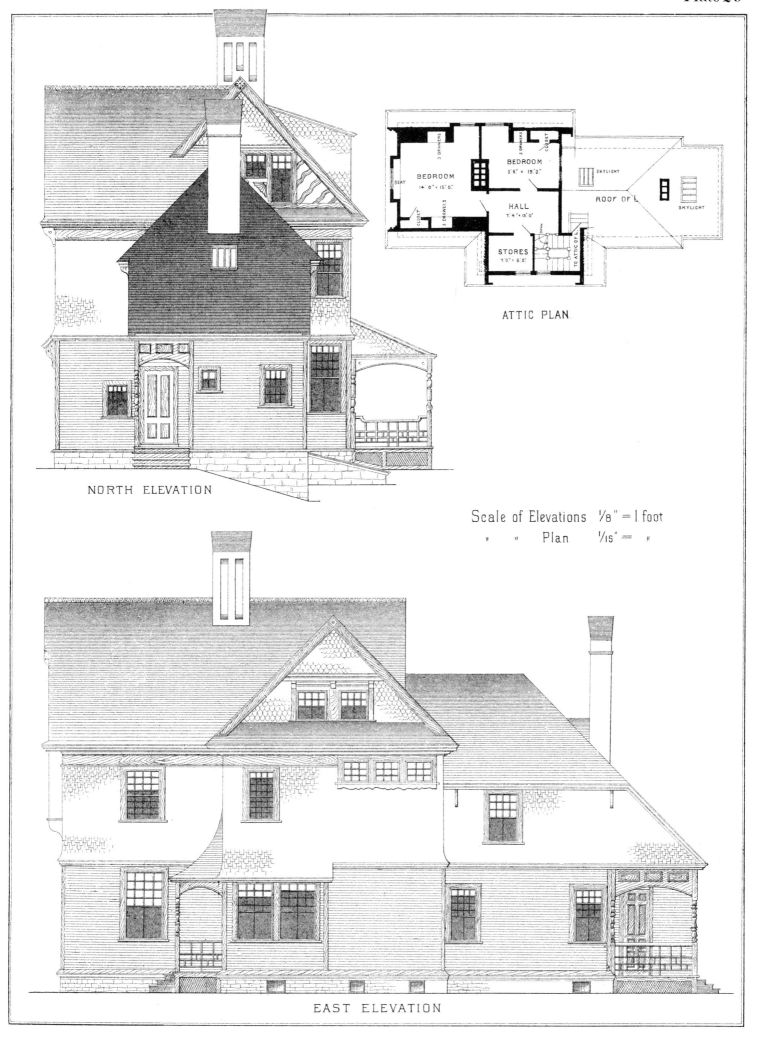

ATTIC PLAN.

NORTH ELEVATION

Scale of Elevations ⅛" = 1 foot
"   "   Plan   ⅟₁₆" =   "

EAST ELEVATION

Plate 30

Details of Front Porch etc. Design Plate 27

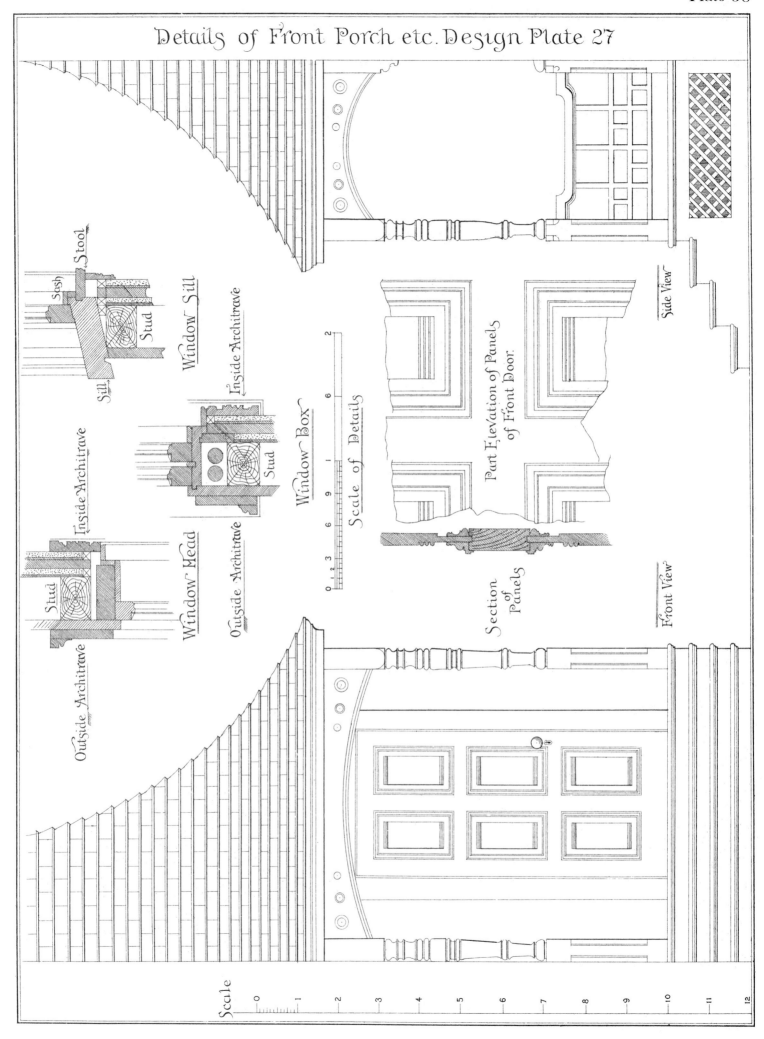

Stool

Sash

Sill

Stud

Window Sill

Inside Architrave

Inside Architrave

Stud

Window Box

Window Head

Stud

Outside Architrave

Outside Architrave

Scale of Details

2

6

1

9

6

3

0 1 2 3

Part Elevation of Panels
of Front Door.

Side View

Section
of
Panels

Front View

Scale

0

1

2

3

4

5

6

7

8

9

10

11

12

Plate 31

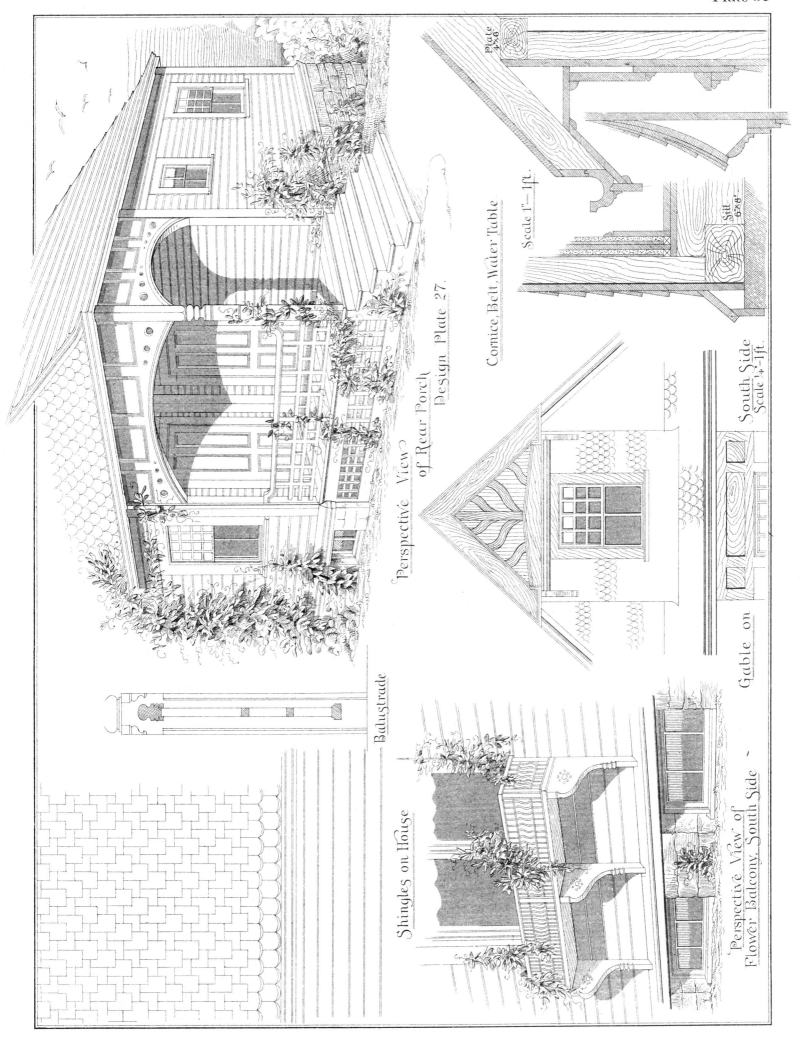

Plate 4×6

Sill 6×8″

Cornice, Belt, Water Table
Scale 1″ = 1ft.

Perspective View
of Rear Porch
Design Plate 27.

South Side
Scale ¼ = 1ft.

Gable on

Balustrade

Shingles on House

Perspective View of
Flower Balcony. South Side

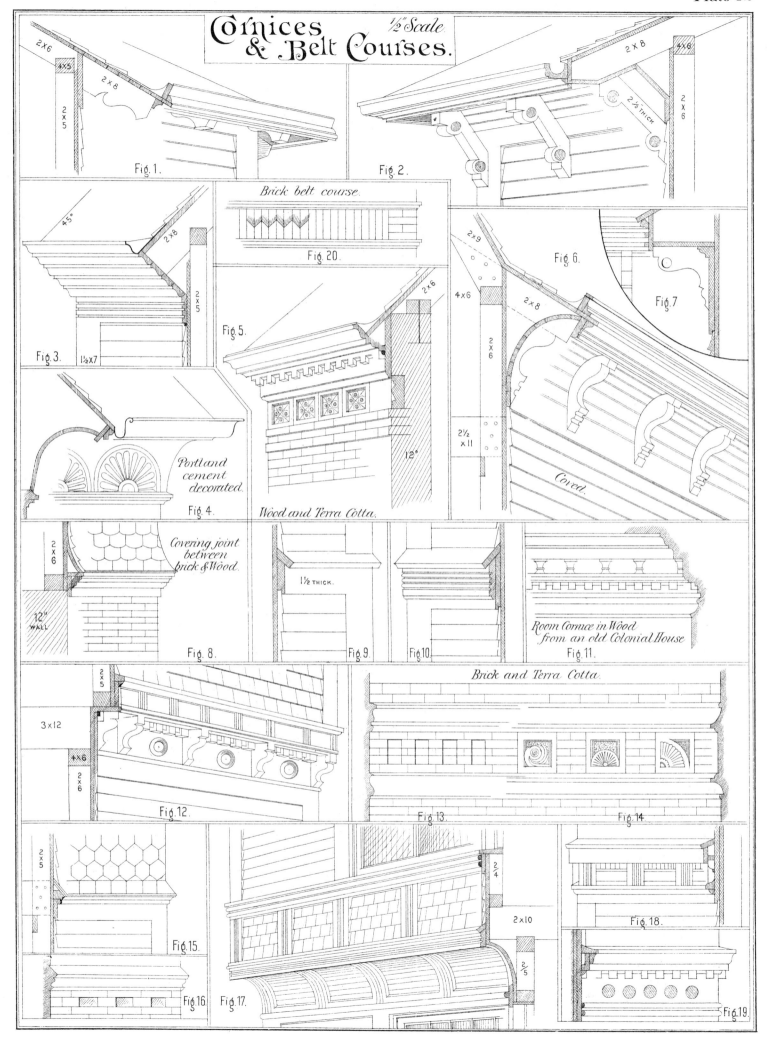

Plate 32

Cornices & Belt Courses.

½" Scale.

Fig. 1.

2×6
4×5
2×5
2×8

Fig. 2.

2×8
4×6
2½" thick
2×6

Fig. 3.

45°
2×8
2×5
1½×7

Brick belt course.

Fig. 20.

Fig. 5.

2×6
2×6
4×6
2×6
2½ ×11
12°

Wood and Terra Cotta.

Fig. 4.

Portland cement decorated.

Fig. 6.

Fig. 7.

2×9
2×8

Coved.

Fig. 8.

Covering joint between brick & wood.

2×6
12" WALL

Fig. 9.

1½ THICK.

Fig. 10.

Fig. 11.

Room Cornice in Wood from an old Colonial House

Fig. 12.

2×5
3×12
4×6
2×6

Brick and Terra Cotta.

Fig. 13.

Fig. 14.

Fig. 15.

2×5

Fig. 16.

Fig. 17.

2/4
2×10
2/5

Fig. 18.

Fig. 19.

Plate 33

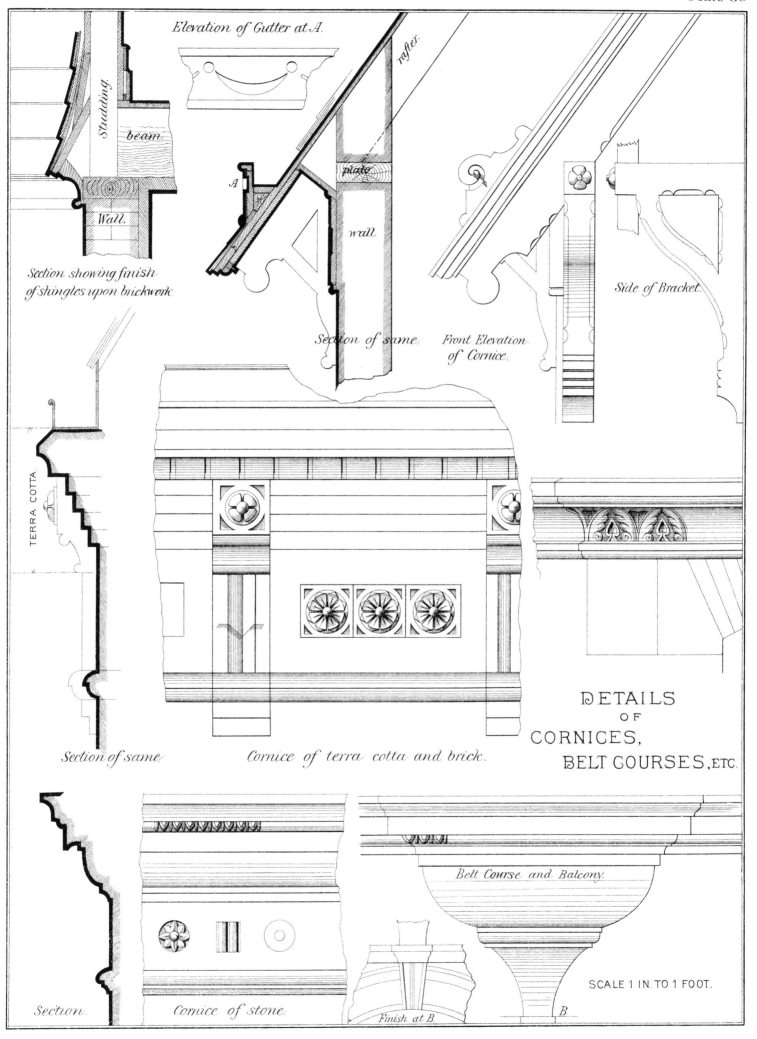

Elevation of Gutter at A.

Studding.

beam

Wall.

Section showing finish
of shingles upon brickwork.

rafter.

plate

A

wall

Section of same.

Front Elevation
of Cornice.

Side of Bracket.

TERRA COTTA.

Section of same.

Cornice of terra cotta and brick.

DETAILS
OF
CORNICES,
BELT COURSES, ETC.

Section.

Cornice of stone.

Finish at B.

Belt Course and Balcony.

B

SCALE 1 IN. TO 1 FOOT.

Plate 34

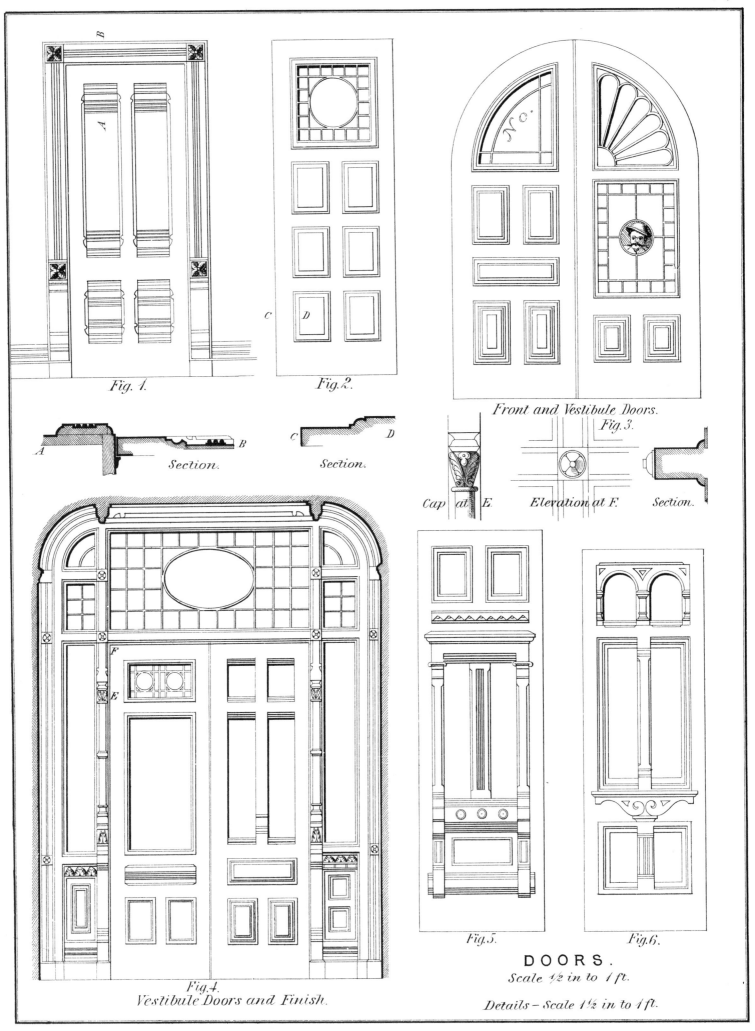

Fig. 1.

Fig. 2.

Front and Vestibule Doors.

Fig. 3.

A Section. B

C Section. D

Cap at E.

Elevation at F.

Section.

Fig. 5.

Fig. 6.

Fig. 4.
Vestibule Doors and Finish.

DOORS.
Scale ½ in to 1 ft.

Details — Scale 1½ in to 1 ft.

Plate 37

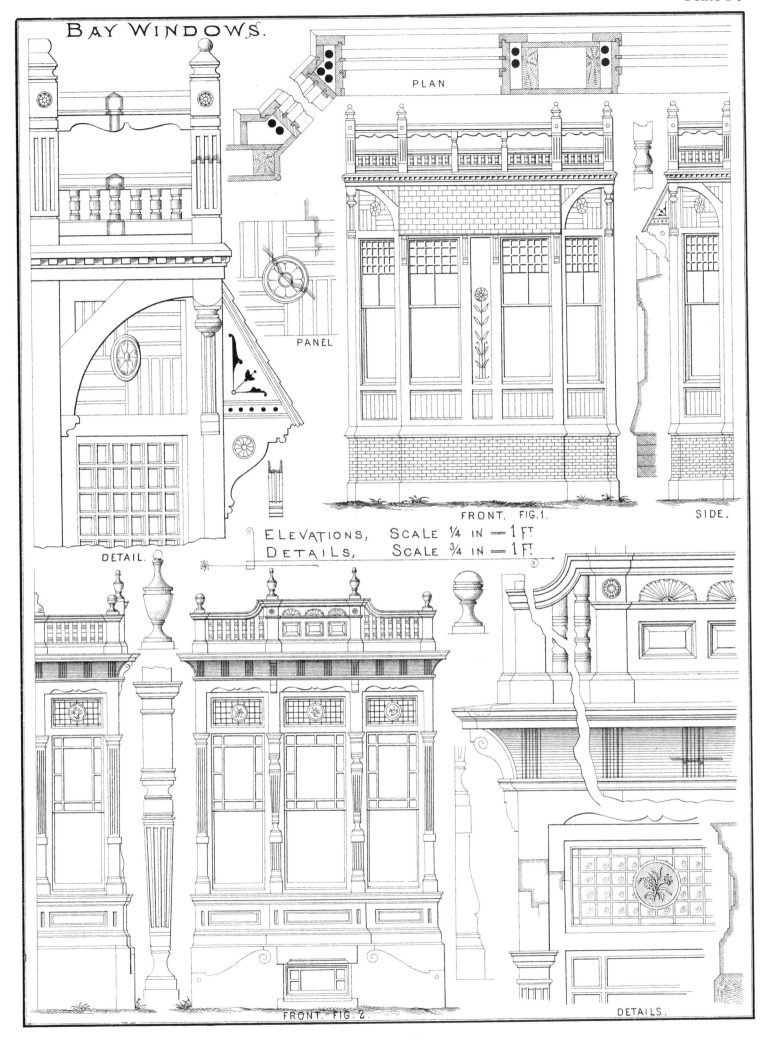

BAY WINDOWS.

PLAN

PANEL

DETAIL.

FRONT. FIG. 1.

SIDE.

ELEVATIONS, SCALE ¼ IN = 1 FT

DETAILS, SCALE ¾ IN = 1 FT

FRONT. FIG. 2.

DETAILS.

Plate 38

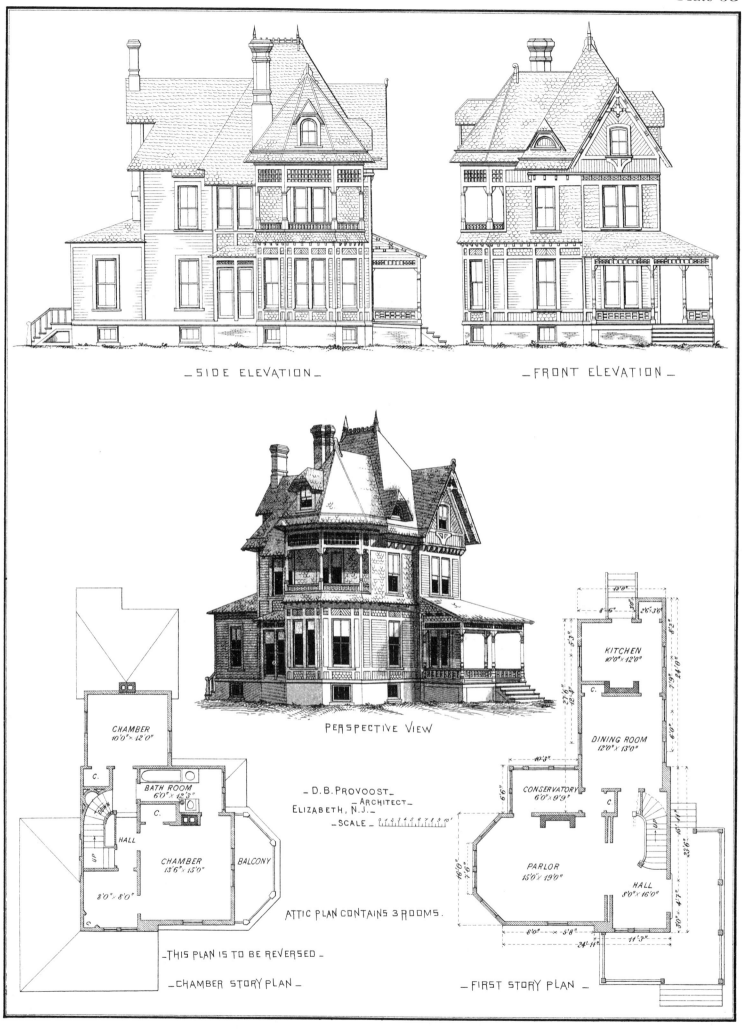

SIDE ELEVATION

FRONT ELEVATION

PERSPECTIVE VIEW

CHAMBER
10'0" x 12'0"

BATH ROOM
6'0" x 12'3"

HALL

CHAMBER
13'6" x 15'0"

BALCONY

8'0" x 8'0"

D.B. PROVOOST
ARCHITECT
ELIZABETH, N.J._
SCALE

ATTIC PLAN CONTAINS 3 ROOMS.

THIS PLAN IS TO BE REVERSED

CHAMBER STORY PLAN

KITCHEN
10'0" x 12'0"

DINING ROOM
12'0" x 13'0"

CONSERVATORY
6'0" x 9'9"

PARLOR
15'0" x 19'0"

HALL
8'0" x 16'0"

FIRST STORY PLAN

Plate 39

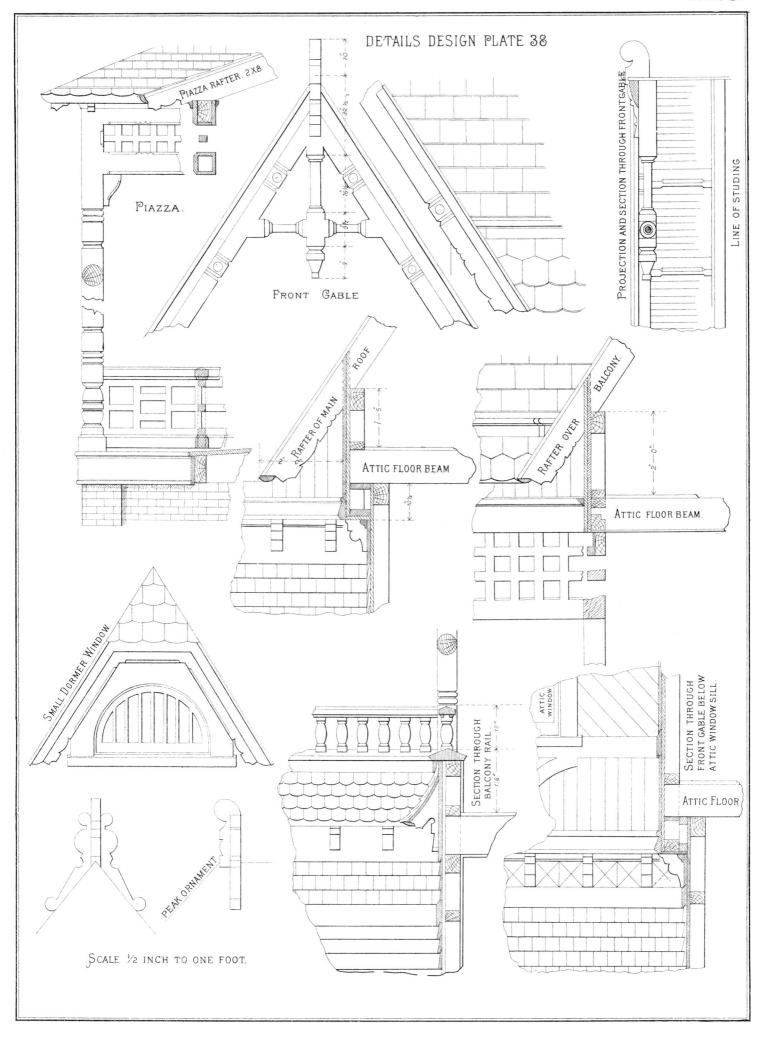

DETAILS DESIGN PLATE 38

PIAZZA.

PIAZZA RAFTER. 2X8

FRONT GABLE

PROJECTION AND SECTION THROUGH FRONT GABLE

LINE OF STUDING

RAFTER OF MAIN ROOF

ATTIC FLOOR BEAM

RAFTER OVER BALCONY.

ATTIC FLOOR BEAM.

SMALL DORMER WINDOW

PEAK ORNAMENT

SCALE ½ INCH TO ONE FOOT.

SECTION THROUGH BALCONY RAIL.

SECTION THROUGH FRONT GABLE BELOW ATTIC WINDOW SILL.

ATTIC WINDOW

ATTIC FLOOR

Plate 40

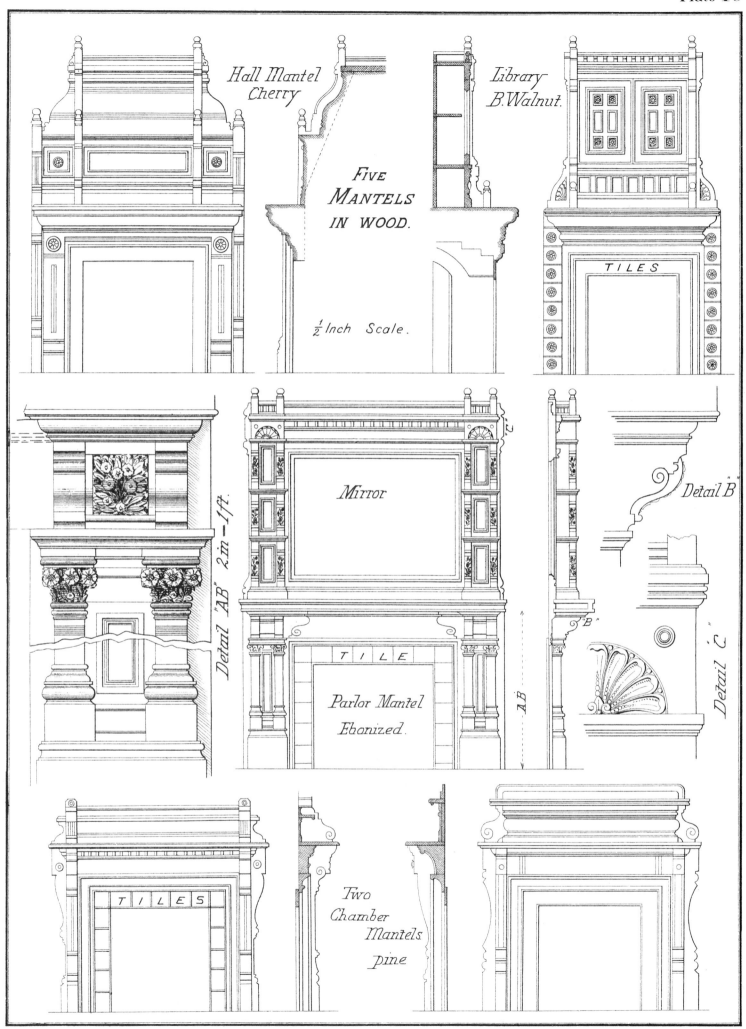

Hall Mantel
Cherry

FIVE
MANTELS
IN WOOD.

½ Inch Scale.

Library
B. Walnut.

TILES

Detail "AB" 2 in = 1 ft.

Mirror

Detail "B"

Detail "C"

TILE

Parlor Mantel
Ebonized.

AB

TILES

Two
Chamber
Mantels
pine

Plate 41

CHAMBER
13'0"X14'0"

DRESS'G
R.

CL.

CHAMBER
13'6"X14'0"

CL.

BATH

BACK HALL

CL.

HALL

BALCONY

CHAMBER
12'0"X14'6"

CL.

CL.

CHAMBER
12'6"X14'6"

HOWE AND DODD, ARCHTS.

BOSTON.

Scale of feet

0   5   10   15   20

DINING ROOM
13'0"X17'10"

CHINA

PANTRY

LIBRARY
9'3"X11'8"

KITCHEN
12'0"X14'6"

UP

HALL

SITTING R.
12'0"X13'6"

DOWN

PORCH

PIAZZA

PARLOR
14'6"X16'0"

PERSPECTIVE VIEW.

Plate 42

East Elevation.

Scale ⅛ in. = 1 ft.

South Elevation.

Plate 43

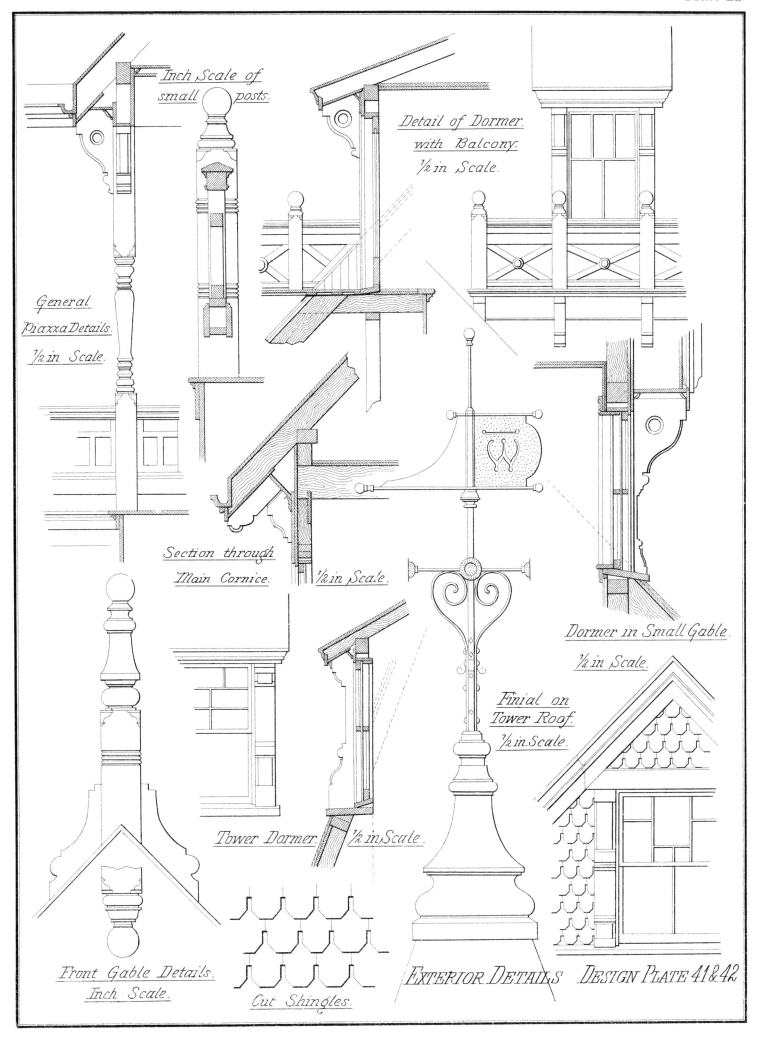

Inch Scale of small posts.

Detail of Dormer with Balcony. ½ in Scale.

General Piazza Details. ½ in Scale.

Section through Main Cornice. ½ in Scale.

Dormer in Small Gable. ½ in Scale.

Finial on Tower Roof. ½ in. Scale.

Tower Dormer. ½ in Scale.

Front Gable Details. Inch Scale.

Cut Shingles.

EXTERIOR DETAILS   DESIGN PLATE 41 & 42

Plate 44

Bracket used on beam between Library & Sitting R.

1½ in = 1ft.

Bracket in Hall.

Inch Scale.

Rosette on Newel.

Roll stopping Hand rail on Newel post.

Stair Newel.

Plaster.

Plaster.

Window Finish etc.

3 in. = 1ft.

Small post.

A

Stair Details rail and balustrade.

Inch Scale.

Bracket A on small posts.

Elevation of staircase.

1½ in. = 1ft.

INTERIOR DETAILS Design Plate 41 & 42.

Plate 45

House at Short Hills, N.J.

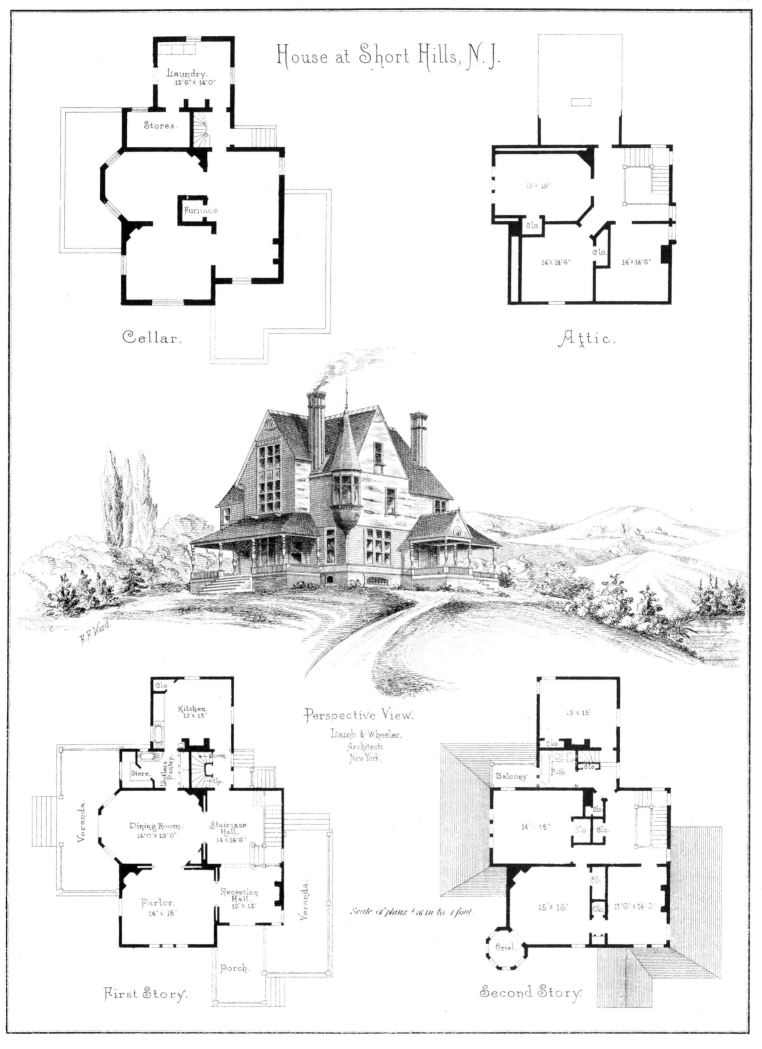

Cellar.

- Laundry. 12'6" x 14'0"
- Stores.
- Furnace

Attic.

- 13' x 19'
- Clo.
- 14' x 14'6"
- Clo.
- 14' x 14'6"

Perspective View.

Lamb & Wheeler,
Architects,
New York.

F.F. Ward.

First Story.

- Clo.
- Kitchen. 13' x 15'
- Store.
- Butler's Pantry.
- Down.
- Up.
- Veranda.
- Dining Room. 14'0" x 19'0"
- Staircase Hall. 14 x 14'6"
- Parlor. 14' x 18'
- Reception Hall. 12' x 13'
- Veranda.
- Porch.

Scale of plans 1/16 in. to 1 foot.

Second Story.

- 13 x 15'
- Clo.
- Clo.
- Balcony
- Bath.
- Clo.
- 14' x 15'
- Clo.
- Clo.
- 15' x 16'
- 11'6" x 14'3"
- Clo.
- Clo.
- Oriel.

Plate 46

Front Elevation.

Scale 1/8 in. to 1 foot.

Side Elevation.

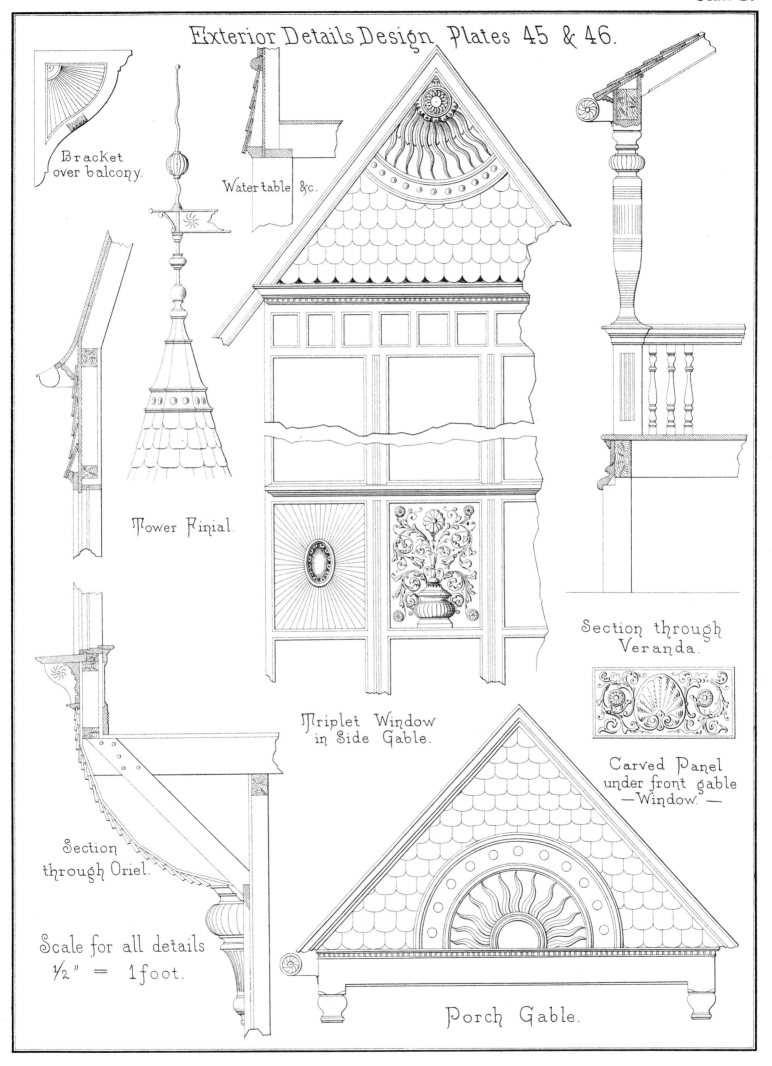

Plate 47

Exterior Details Design Plates 45 & 46.

Bracket over balcony.

Watertable &c.

Tower Finial.

Section through Oriel.

Scale for all details
½" = 1 foot.

Triplet Window in Side Gable.

Section through Veranda.

Carved Panel under front gable
— Window. —

Porch Gable.

Plate 48

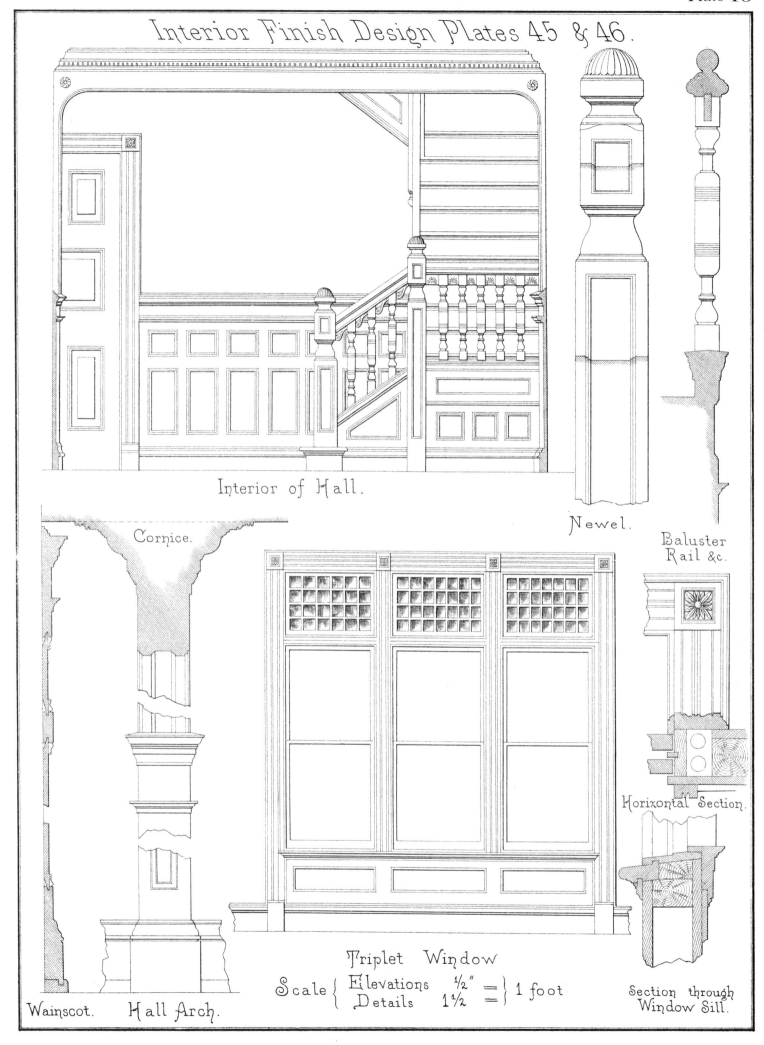

Interior Finish Design Plates 45 & 46.

Interior of Hall.

Newel.

Cornice.

Baluster Rail &c.

Horixontal Section.

Triplet Window

Scale { Elevations ½" = } 1 foot
        Details 1½ =

Section through Window Sill.

Wainscot. Hall Arch.

Plate 49

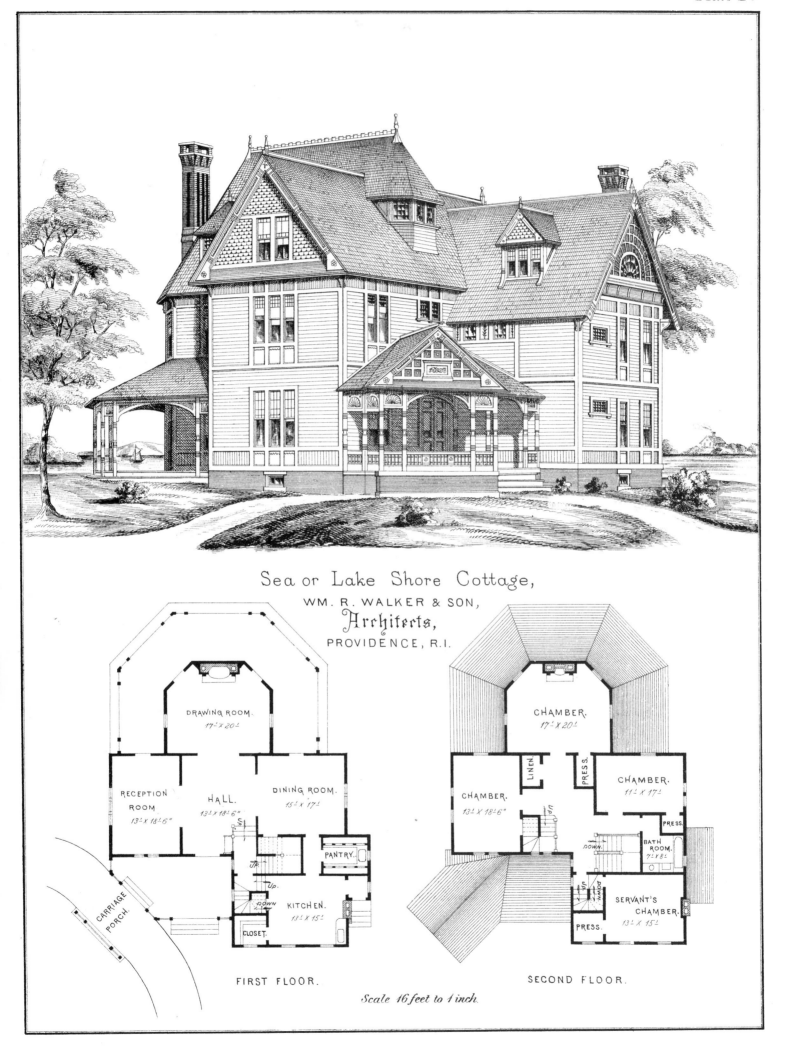

Sea or Lake Shore Cottage,

WM. R. WALKER & SON,

Architects,

PROVIDENCE, R.I.

FIRST FLOOR.

DRAWING ROOM.
17¹ X 20¹

RECEPTION ROOM
13¹ X 18¹ 6"

HALL.
13¹ X 18¹ 6"

DINING ROOM.
15¹ X 17¹

PANTRY.

UP.

UP.

DOWN

KITCHEN.
13¹ X 15¹

CLOSET.

CARRIAGE PORCH.

SECOND FLOOR.

CHAMBER.
17¹ X 20¹

CHAMBER.
13¹ X 18¹ 6"

LINEN.

PRESS.

CHAMBER.
11¹ X 17¹

PRESS.

BATH ROOM.
7¹ X 8¹

UP.

DOWN.

DOWN.

SERVANT'S CHAMBER.
13¹ X 15¹

PRESS.

Scale 16 feet to 1 inch.

Plate 50

SEA OR LAKE SHORE COTTAGE.

WATER FRONT.

SIDE ELEVATION.

Scale 10 ft. to 1 in.

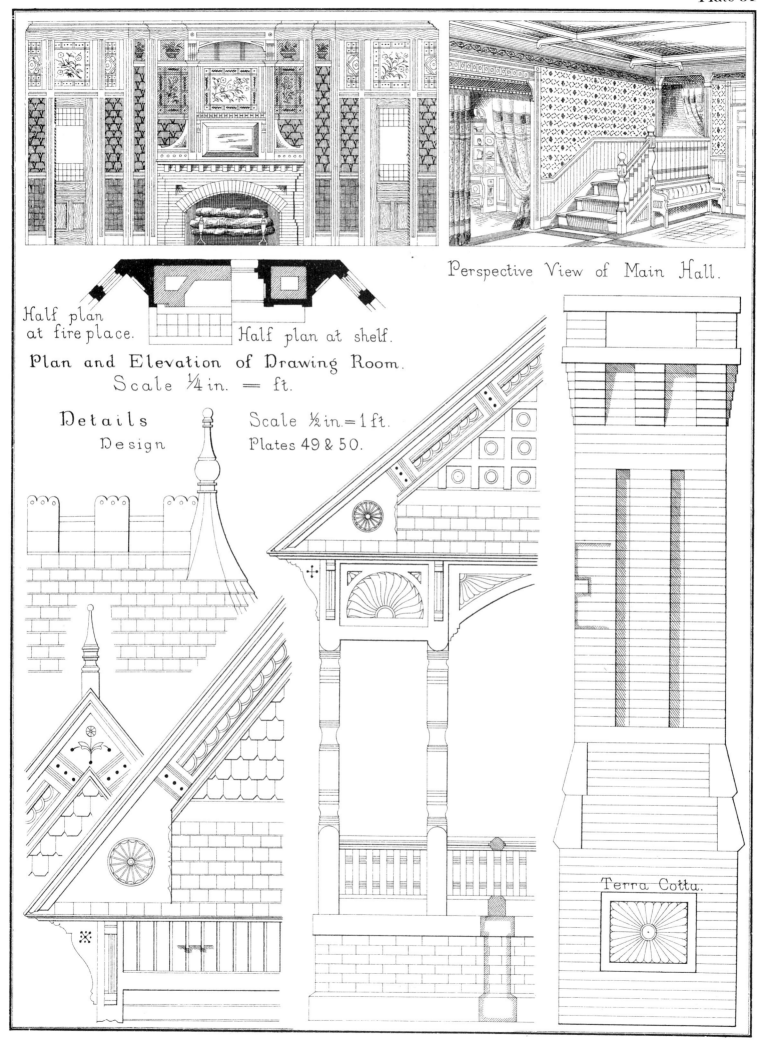

Plate 51

Perspective View of Main Hall.

Half plan
at fire place.

Half plan at shelf.

Plan and Elevation of Drawing Room.
Scale ¼ in. = ft.

Details
Design

Scale ½ in. = 1 ft.
Plates 49 & 50.

Terra Cotta.

Plate 52

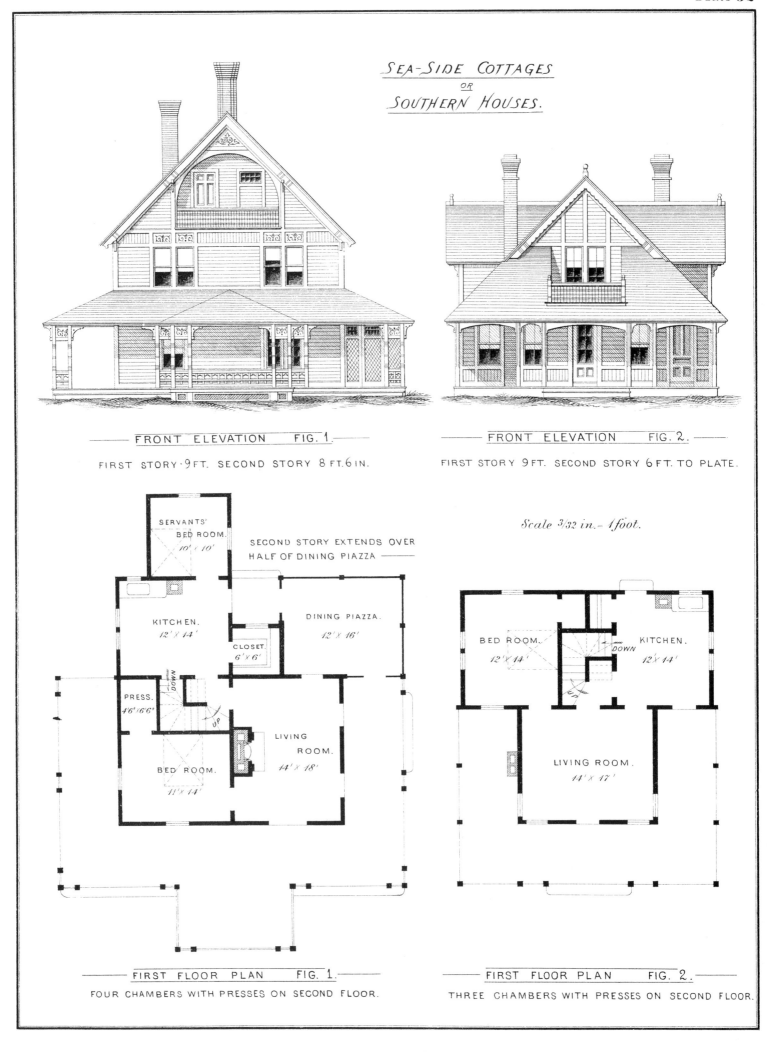

Sea-Side Cottages
_or_
Southern Houses.

FRONT ELEVATION   FIG. 1.

FIRST STORY 9 FT. SECOND STORY 8 FT. 6 IN.

FRONT ELEVATION   FIG. 2.

FIRST STORY 9 FT. SECOND STORY 6 FT. TO PLATE.

SECOND STORY EXTENDS OVER
HALF OF DINING PIAZZA

Scale 3/32 in. = 1 foot.

SERVANTS'
BED ROOM.
10' X 10'

KITCHEN.
12' X 14'

DINING PIAZZA.
12' X 16'

CLOSET.
6' X 6'

DOWN

PRESS.
4'6" X 6'6"

UP

LIVING
ROOM.
14' X 18'

BED ROOM.
11' X 14'

BED ROOM.
12' X 14'

DOWN

KITCHEN.
12' X 14'

UP

LIVING ROOM.
14' X 17'

FIRST FLOOR PLAN   FIG. 1.

FOUR CHAMBERS WITH PRESSES ON SECOND FLOOR.

FIRST FLOOR PLAN   FIG. 2.

THREE CHAMBERS WITH PRESSES ON SECOND FLOOR.

Plate 53

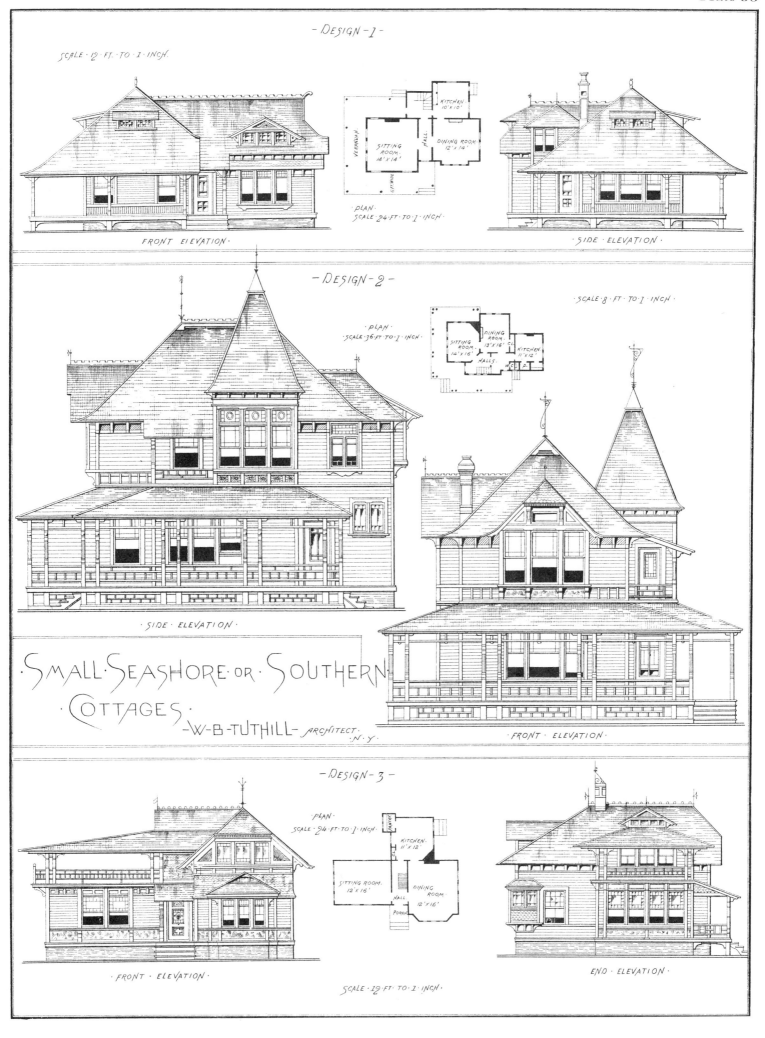

- DESIGN - 1 -

SCALE · 12 · FT · TO · 1 · INCH.

KITCHEN
10' X 10'

SITTING
ROOM
14' X 14'

DINING ROOM
12' X 14'

HALL

VERANDAH

6 FT · WIDE

PLAN
SCALE · 24 · FT · TO · 1 · INCH.

FRONT · ELEVATION ·

SIDE · ELEVATION ·

- DESIGN - 2 -

PLAN
SCALE · 36 · FT · TO · 1 · INCH.

SCALE · 8 · FT · TO · 1 · INCH.

SITTING
ROOM
14' X 16'

DINING
ROOM
13' X 16'

KITCHEN
11' X 12'

HALLS

CL.

W.C.

· SIDE · ELEVATION ·

· FRONT · ELEVATION ·

SMALL · SEASHORE · OR · SOUTHERN ·
COTTAGES · —W·B·TUTHILL— ARCHITECT
N·Y

- DESIGN - 3 -

PLAN
SCALE · 24 · FT · TO · 1 · INCH.

PANTRY

KITCHEN
11' X 12'

SITTING ROOM
12' X 16'

DINING
ROOM
12' X 16'

HALL

PORCH

· FRONT · ELEVATION ·

END · ELEVATION ·

SCALE · 12 · FT · TO · 1 · INCH.

Plate 54

LATTICE WORK.

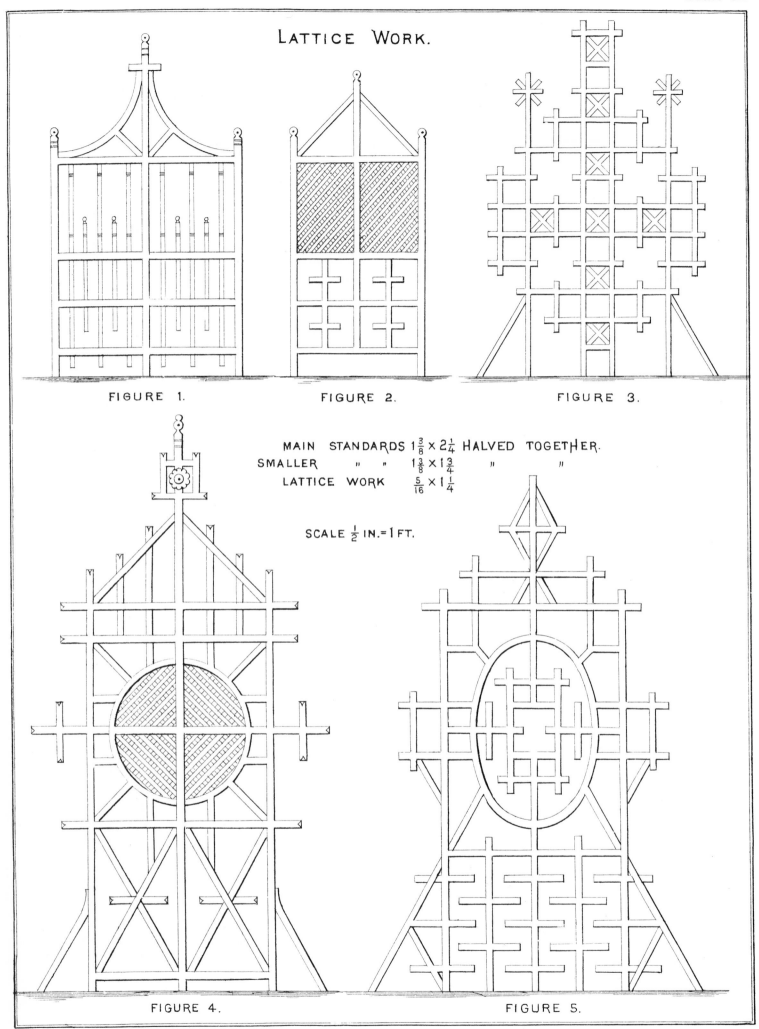

FIGURE 1.

FIGURE 2.

FIGURE 3.

MAIN STANDARDS $1\frac{3}{8} \times 2\frac{1}{4}$ HALVED TOGETHER.
SMALLER " " $1\frac{3}{8} \times 1\frac{3}{4}$ " "
LATTICE WORK $\frac{5}{16} \times 1\frac{1}{4}$

SCALE $\frac{1}{2}$ IN.= 1 FT.

FIGURE 4.

FIGURE 5.

Plate 55

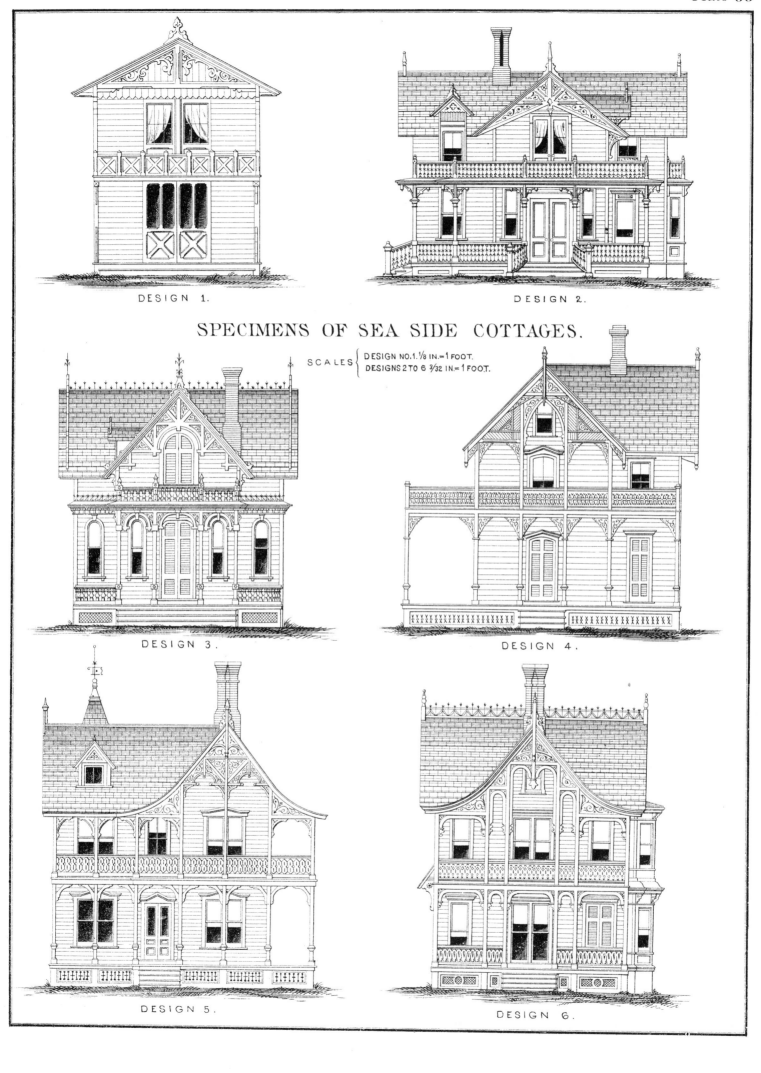

DESIGN 1.

DESIGN 2.

SPECIMENS OF SEA SIDE COTTAGES.

SCALES { DESIGN NO.1. ⅛ IN.=1 FOOT.
DESIGNS 2 TO 6 ³/₃₂ IN.=1 FOOT.

DESIGN 3.

DESIGN 4.

DESIGN 5.

DESIGN 6.

Plate 56

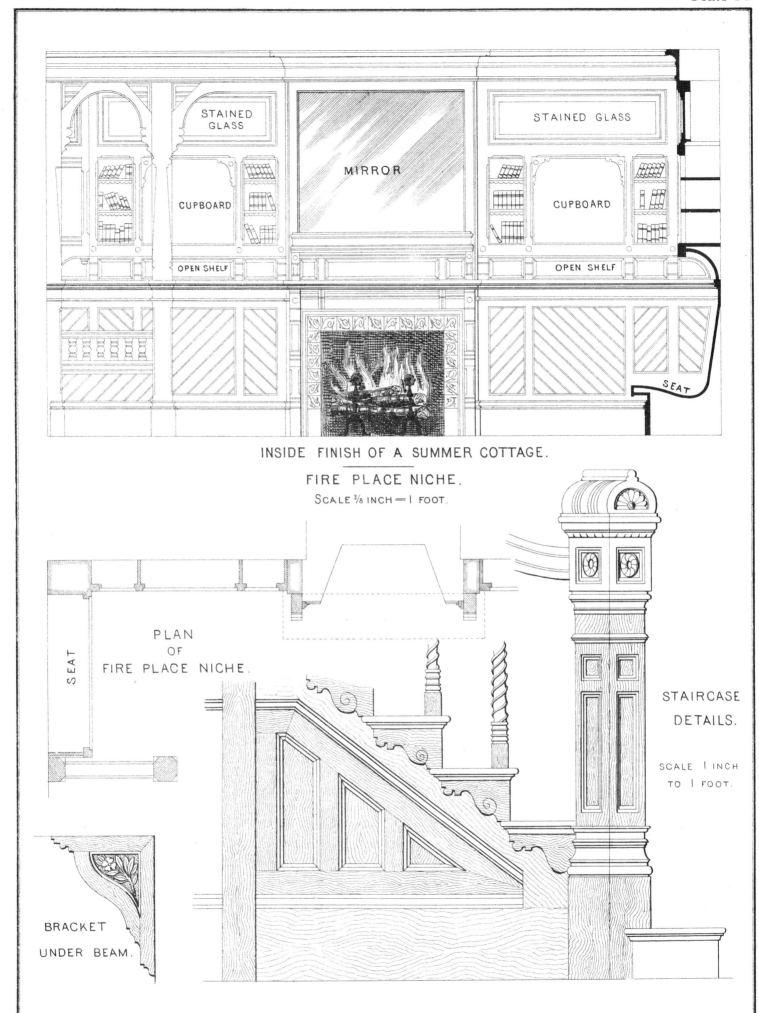

INSIDE FINISH OF A SUMMER COTTAGE.

FIRE PLACE NICHE.

SCALE ⅜ INCH = 1 FOOT.

STAINED GLASS

STAINED GLASS

MIRROR

CUPBOARD

CUPBOARD

OPEN SHELF

OPEN SHELF

SEAT

PLAN
OF
FIRE PLACE NICHE.

SEAT

STAIRCASE
DETAILS.

SCALE 1 INCH
TO 1 FOOT.

BRACKET
UNDER BEAM.

Plate 57

LAKE VIEW COTTAGE.

J. P. Putnam, Archt.
Boston, Mass.

NORTH ELEVATION.

Scale ⅛ in = 1 ft.

FRONT ELEVATION.

Plate 58

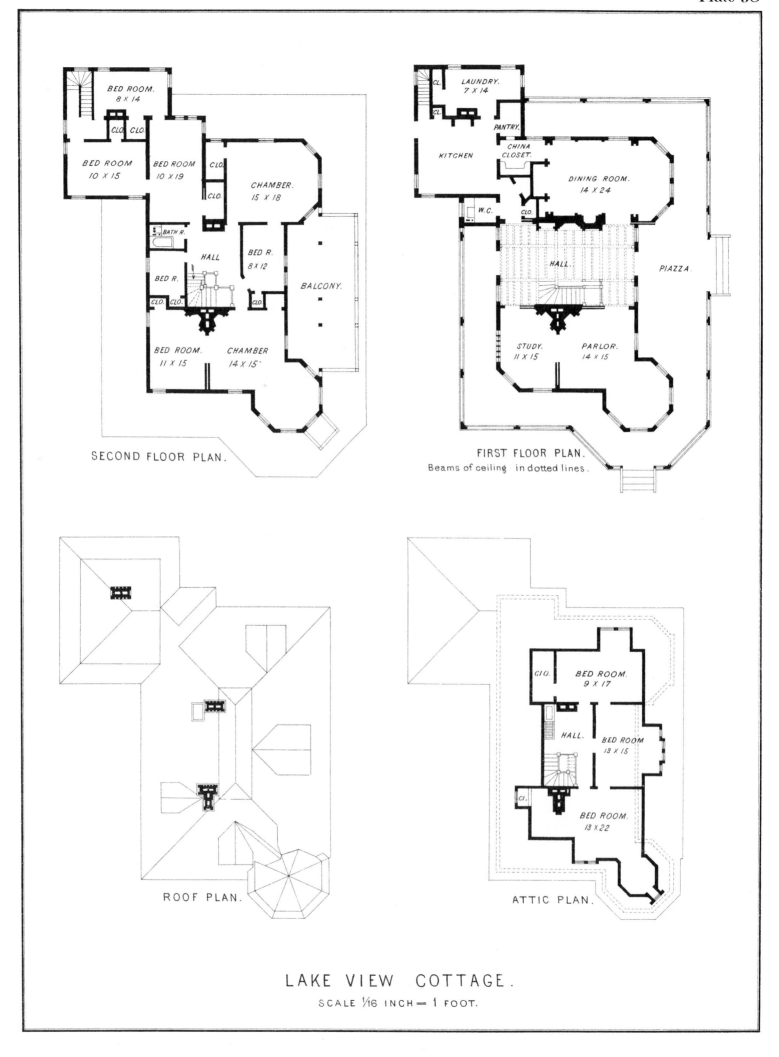

BED ROOM.
8 X 14

CLO. CLO.

BED ROOM
10 X 15

BED ROOM
10 X 19

CLO.

CLO.

CHAMBER.
15 X 18

BATH R.

HALL

BED R.
8 X 12

BED R.

CLO. CLO.

CLO.

BALCONY.

BED ROOM.
11 X 15

CHAMBER
14 X 15

SECOND FLOOR PLAN.

CL.

LAUNDRY.
7 X 14

CL.

PANTRY.

KITCHEN

CHINA CLOSET.

DINING ROOM.
14 X 24

W. C.

CLO.

HALL.

PIAZZA.

STUDY.
11 X 15

PARLOR.
14 X 15

FIRST FLOOR PLAN.
Beams of ceiling in dotted lines.

ROOF PLAN.

CLO.

BED ROOM.
9 X 17

HALL.

BED ROOM
13 X 15

CI.

BED ROOM.
13 X 22

ATTIC PLAN.

LAKE VIEW COTTAGE.
SCALE 1/16 INCH = 1 FOOT.

Plate 59

LAKE VIEW COTTAGE.

SOUTH
ELEVATION.

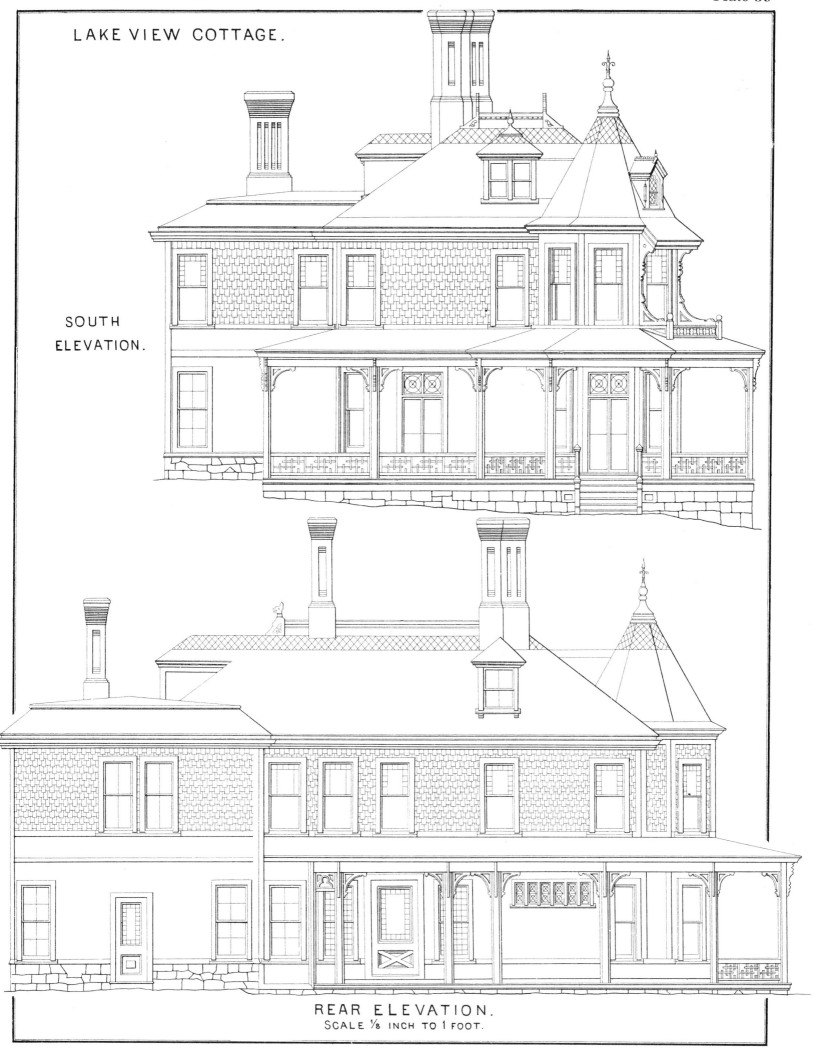

REAR ELEVATION.
SCALE ⅛ INCH TO 1 FOOT.

Plate 60

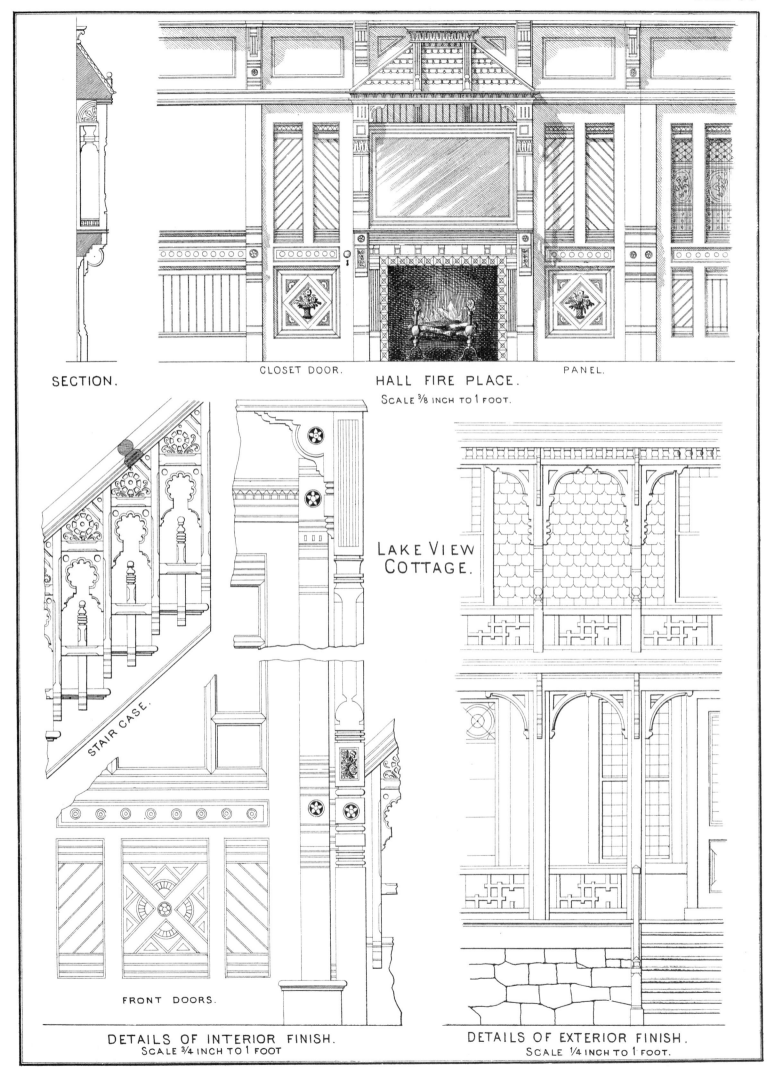

SECTION.

CLOSET DOOR.

HALL FIRE PLACE.
Scale ⅜ inch to 1 foot.

PANEL.

STAIR CASE.

LAKE VIEW COTTAGE.

FRONT DOORS.

DETAILS OF INTERIOR FINISH.
Scale ¾ inch to 1 foot

DETAILS OF EXTERIOR FINISH.
Scale ¼ inch to 1 foot.

Plate 61

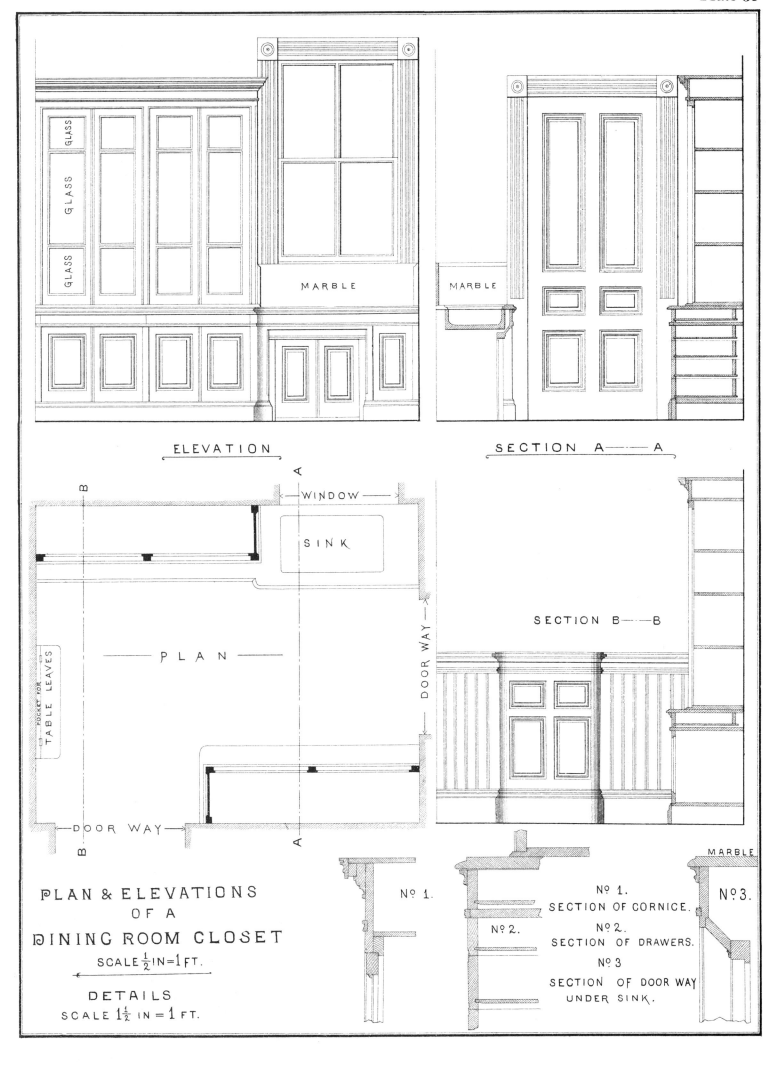

ELEVATION

SECTION A — A

GLASS
GLASS
GLASS
GLASS

MARBLE

MARBLE

B

WINDOW

SINK

PLAN

POCKET FOR
TABLE LEAVES

DOOR WAY

DOOR WAY

A

A

B

SECTION B — B

PLAN & ELEVATIONS
OF A
DINING ROOM CLOSET
SCALE ½ IN = 1 FT.

DETAILS
SCALE 1½ IN = 1 FT.

Nº 1.

Nº 2.

MARBLE

Nº 3.

Nº 1.
SECTION OF CORNICE.

Nº 2.
SECTION OF DRAWERS.

Nº 3
SECTION OF DOOR WAY
UNDER SINK.

Plate 62

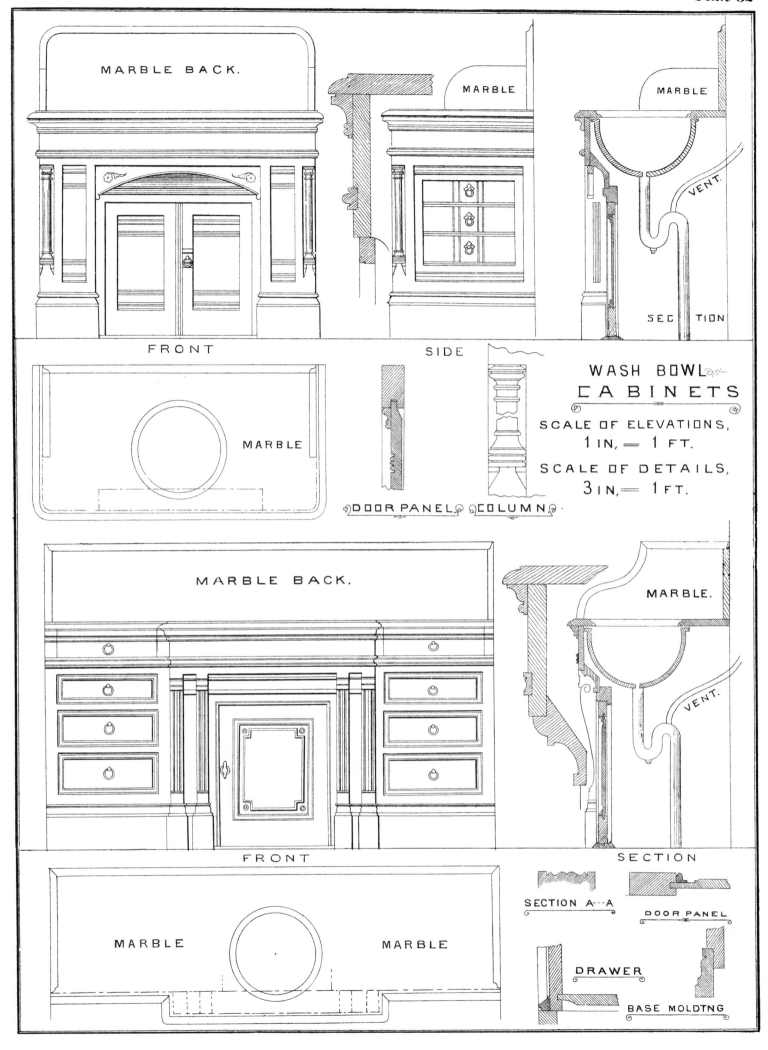

MARBLE BACK.

MARBLE

MARBLE

VENT.

SECTION

FRONT

SIDE

MARBLE

DOOR PANEL

COLUMN

WASH BOWL
CABINETS

SCALE OF ELEVATIONS,
1 IN. = 1 FT.

SCALE OF DETAILS,
3 IN. = 1 FT.

MARBLE BACK.

MARBLE.

VENT.

FRONT

SECTION

SECTION A—A

DOOR PANEL

MARBLE

MARBLE

DRAWER

BASE MOLDING

Plate 63

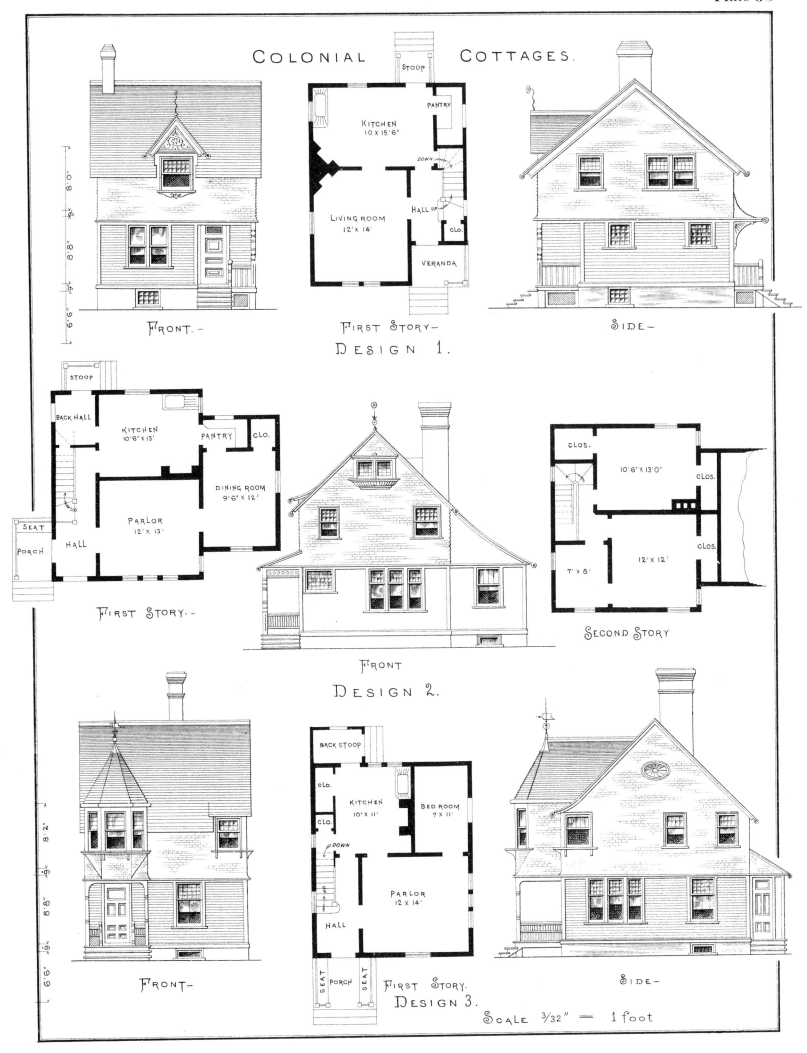

COLONIAL COTTAGES.

STOOP

PANTRY

KITCHEN
10 x 15'6"

DOWN

LIVING ROOM
12' x 14'

HALL UP

CLO.

VERANDA

FRONT.

FIRST STORY.

SIDE.

DESIGN 1.

STOOP

BACK HALL

KITCHEN
10'6" x 13'

PANTRY   CLO.

DINING ROOM
9'6" x 12'

PARLOR
12' x 13'

SEAT

PORCH   HALL

FIRST STORY.

CLOS.

10'6" x 13'0"

CLOS.

CLOS.

7' x 8'

12' x 12'

FRONT

SECOND STORY

DESIGN 2.

BACK STOOP

CLO.

KITCHEN
10' x 11'

BED ROOM
7 x 11'

CLO.

DOWN

PARLOR
12 x 14'

HALL

SEAT   PORCH   SEAT

FRONT

FIRST STORY.

SIDE.

DESIGN 3.

Scale 3/32" = 1 foot

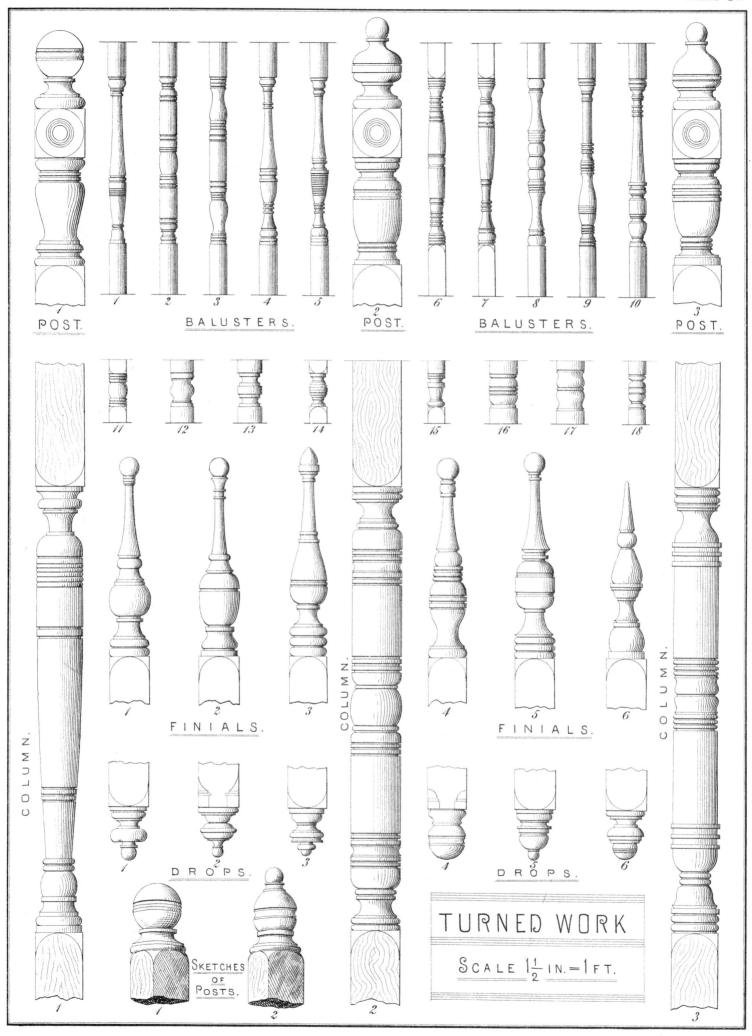

Plate 64

POST.

BALUSTERS.

POST.

BALUSTERS.

POST.

COLUMN.

FINIALS.

COLUMN.

FINIALS.

COLUMN.

DROPS.

DROPS.

SKETCHES OF POSTS.

TURNED WORK

SCALE $1\frac{1}{2}$ IN. = 1 FT.

Plate 65

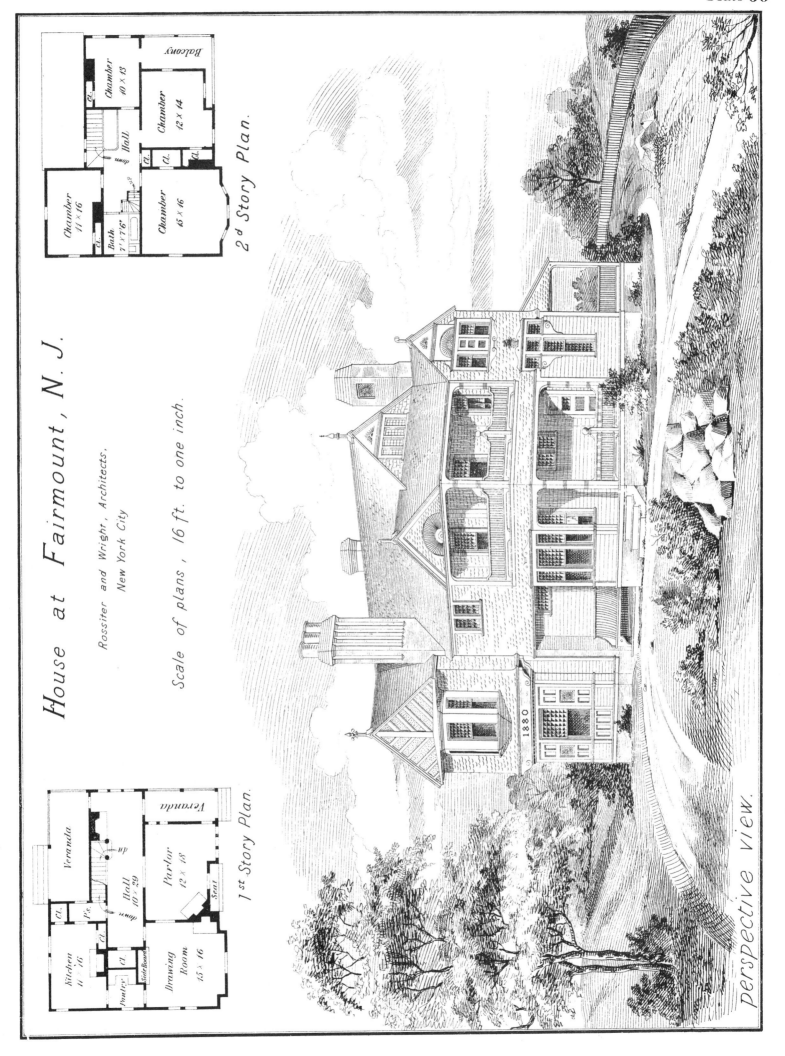

House at Fairmount, N. J.

Rossiter and Wright, Architects.
New York City

Scale of plans, 16 ft. to one inch.

2ᵈ Story Plan.

Chamber 11 × 16

Bath 7'×7'6"

Chamber 15 × 16

Hall

Chamber 11 × 16

Chamber 12 × 14

Chamber 10 × 13

Balcony

1ˢᵗ Story Plan.

Kitchen 11 × 16

Pantry

SideBoard

Drawing Room 15 × 16

Veranda

Hall 10 × 29

Parlor 12 × 18

Seat

Veranda

1880

perspective view.

Plate 66

Front.

House at Fairmount, N.J

Scale 8 feet to 1 inch.

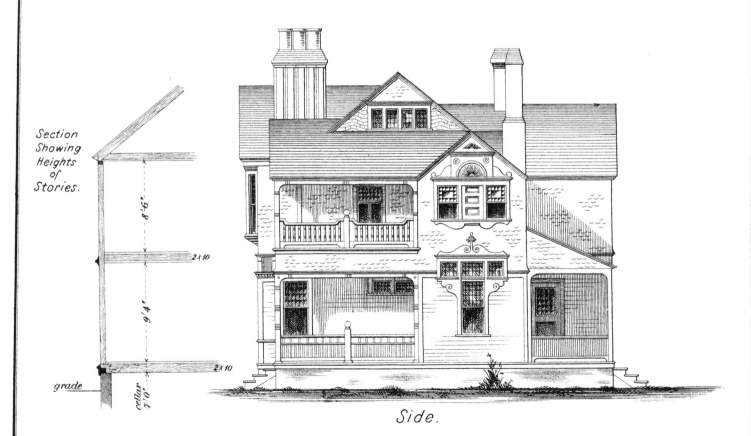

Section
Showing
Heights
of
Stories.

8'6"

2 x 10

9'4"

2 x 10

grade

cellar 7'0"

Side.

Plate 67

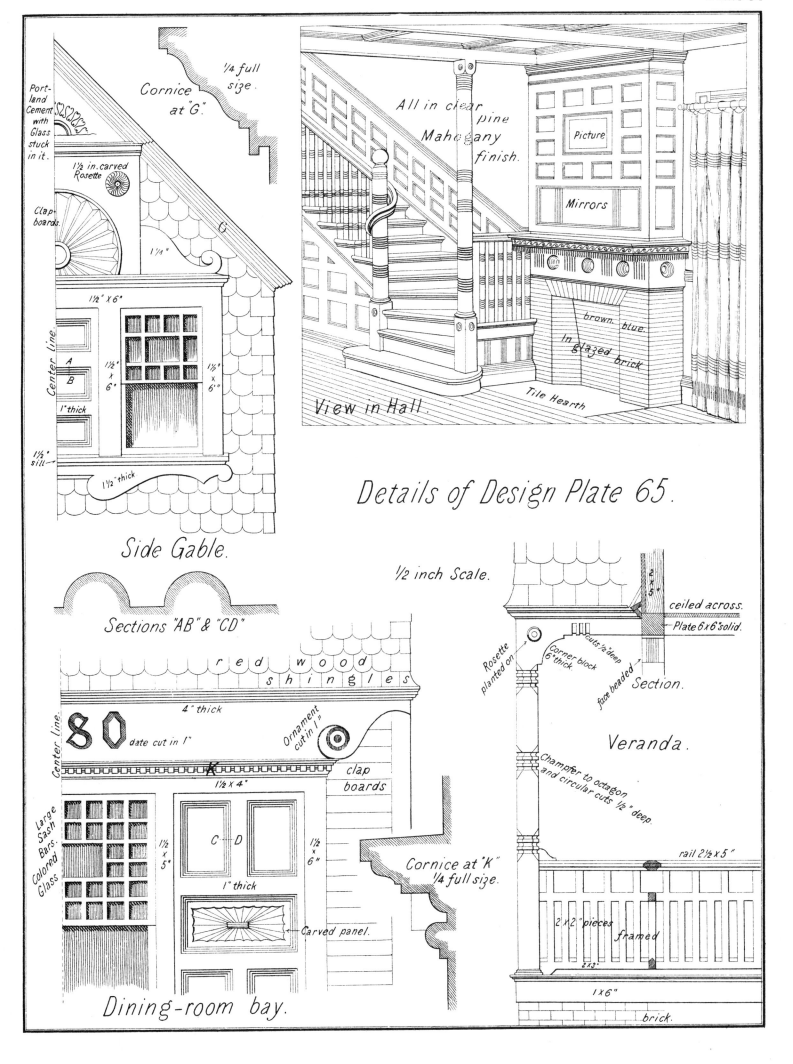

Portland Cement with Glass stuck in it.

Cornice at "G".

¼ full size.

1½ in. carved Rosette

Clapboards.

G

1¼"

Center line.

1½" x 6"

A
B

1½" x 6"

1⅛" x 6"

1" thick

1½" sill

1½" thick.

Side Gable.

All in clear pine Mahogany finish.

Picture

Mirrors

brown. blue.

In glazed brick

Tile Hearth

View in Hall.

Details of Design Plate 65.

½ inch Scale.

Sections "AB" & "CD"

red wood shingles

4" thick

Center line.

80 date cut in 1"

Ornament cut in 1"

K

1½ x 4"

clap boards

Large Sash Bars. Colored Glass

C D

1½ x 5"

1" thick

1½ x 6"

Carved panel.

Cornice at "K" ¼ full size.

Dining-room bay.

ceiled across.
Plate 6x6 solid.

2 x 5

Rosette planted on

Corner block 6" thick

cuts ½" deep

face beaded

Section.

Veranda.

Chamfer to octagon and circular cuts ½" deep.

rail 2½ x 5"

2 x 2" pieces framed

2 x 3"

1 x 6"

brick.

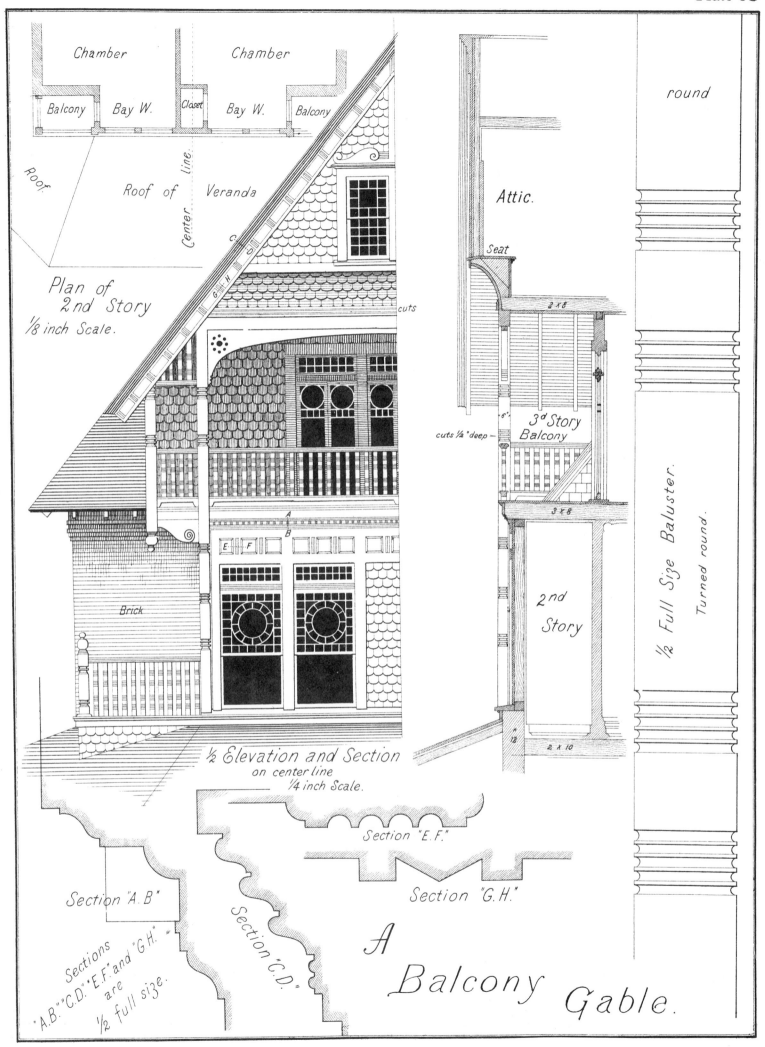

Plate 68

Chamber   Chamber

Balcony Bay W. Closet Bay W. Balcony

Roof.

Roof of   Veranda

Center line

Plan of
2nd Story
⅛ inch Scale.

round

Attic.

Seat

cuts

cuts ½" deep

3d Story
Balcony

2×8

½ Full Size Baluster.
Turned round.

2nd
Story

Brick

A
B

E F

½ Elevation and Section
on center line
¼ inch Scale.

3×8

2×10

Section "E.F."

Section "G.H."

Section "A.B"

Section "C.D."

Sections
"A.B""C.D.""E.F."and "G.H."
are
½ full size.

A
Balcony Gable.

Plate 69

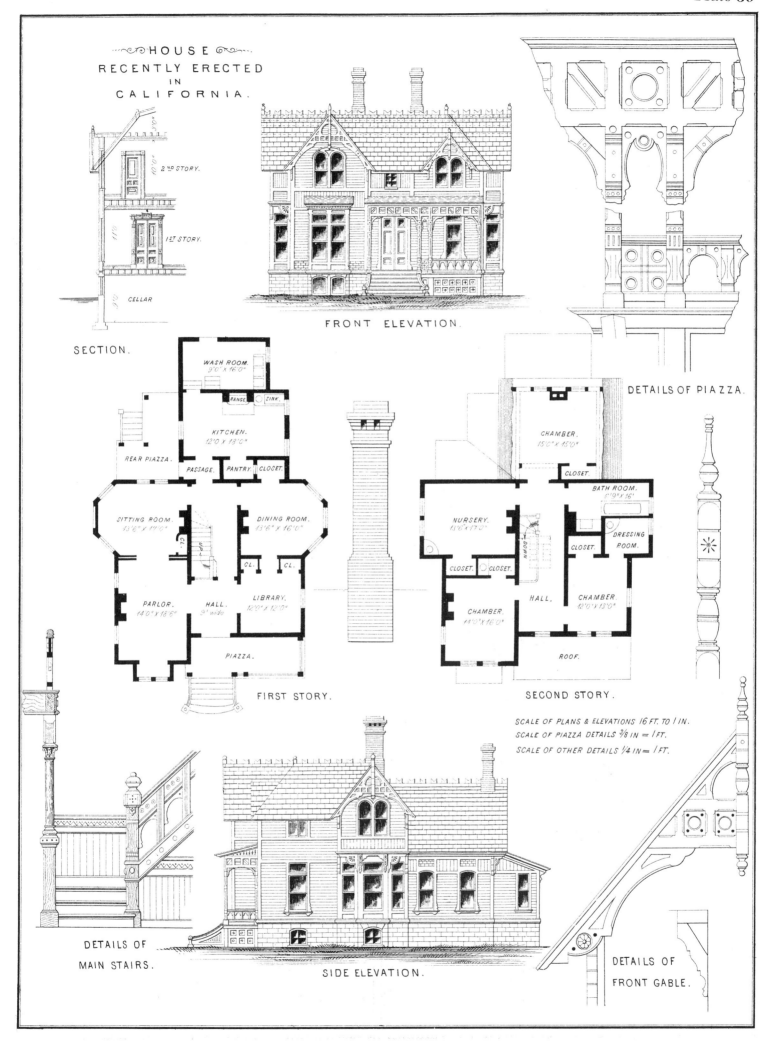

HOUSE
RECENTLY ERECTED
IN
CALIFORNIA.

SECTION.

2ND STORY.
1ST STORY.
CELLAR

FRONT ELEVATION.

DETAILS OF PIAZZA.

WASH ROOM.
9'0" X 16'0"

RANGE   SINK.

KITCHEN.
12'0" X 18'0"

REAR PIAZZA.

PASSAGE   PANTRY.   CLOSET.

SITTING ROOM.
13'6" X 19'6"

DINING ROOM.
13'6" X 16'0"

CL.   CL.

PARLOR.
14'0" X 18'6"

HALL.
9' wide

LIBRARY.
12'0" X 12'0"

PIAZZA.

FIRST STORY.

CHAMBER.
15'0" X 15'0"

CLOSET.

BATH ROOM.
6'9" X 16'

NURSERY.
13'6" X 17'0"

DRESSING ROOM.

CLOSET.

CLOSET.   CLOSET.

DOWN

HALL.

CHAMBER.
13'0" X 13'0"

CHAMBER.
14'0" X 16'0"

ROOF.

SECOND STORY.

SCALE OF PLANS & ELEVATIONS 16 FT. TO 1 IN.
SCALE OF PIAZZA DETAILS 3/8 IN = 1 FT.
SCALE OF OTHER DETAILS 1/4 IN = 1 FT.

DETAILS OF
MAIN STAIRS.

SIDE ELEVATION.

DETAILS OF
FRONT GABLE.

Plate 70

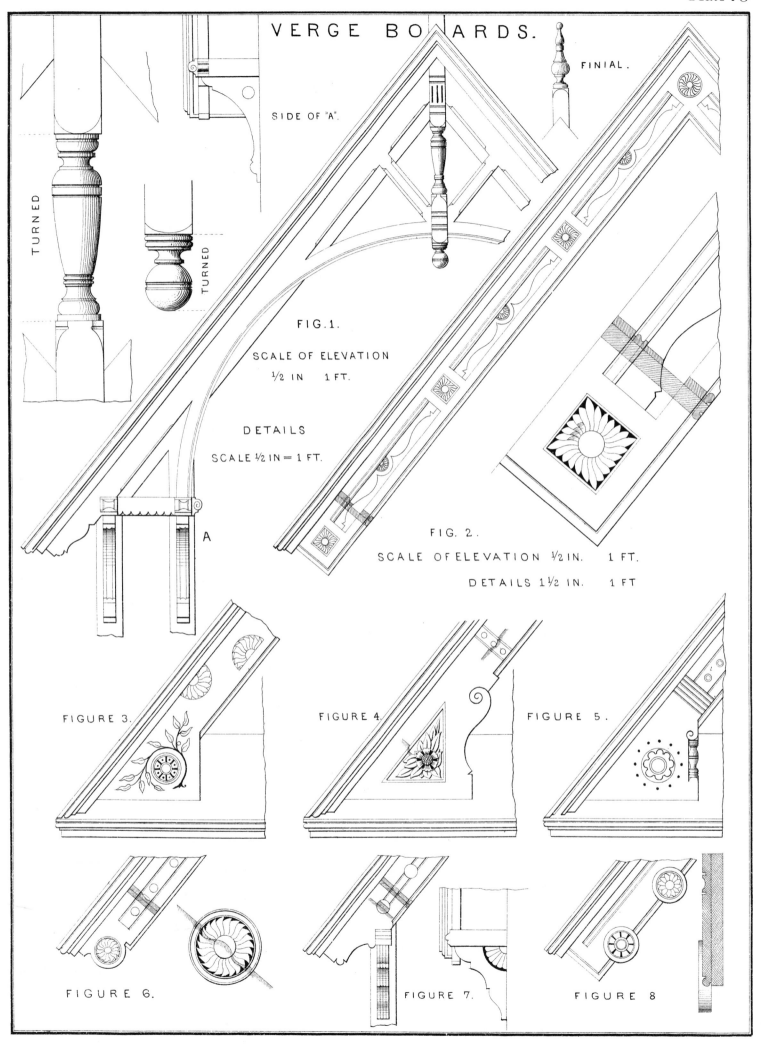

VERGE BOARDS.

SIDE OF "A".

FINIAL.

TURNED

TURNED

FIG. 1.

SCALE OF ELEVATION
½ IN   1 FT.

DETAILS

SCALE ½ IN = 1 FT.

A

FIG. 2.

SCALE OF ELEVATION ½ IN.   1 FT.

DETAILS 1½ IN.   1 FT

FIGURE 3.

FIGURE 4.

FIGURE 5.

FIGURE 6.

FIGURE 7.

FIGURE 8

Plate 71

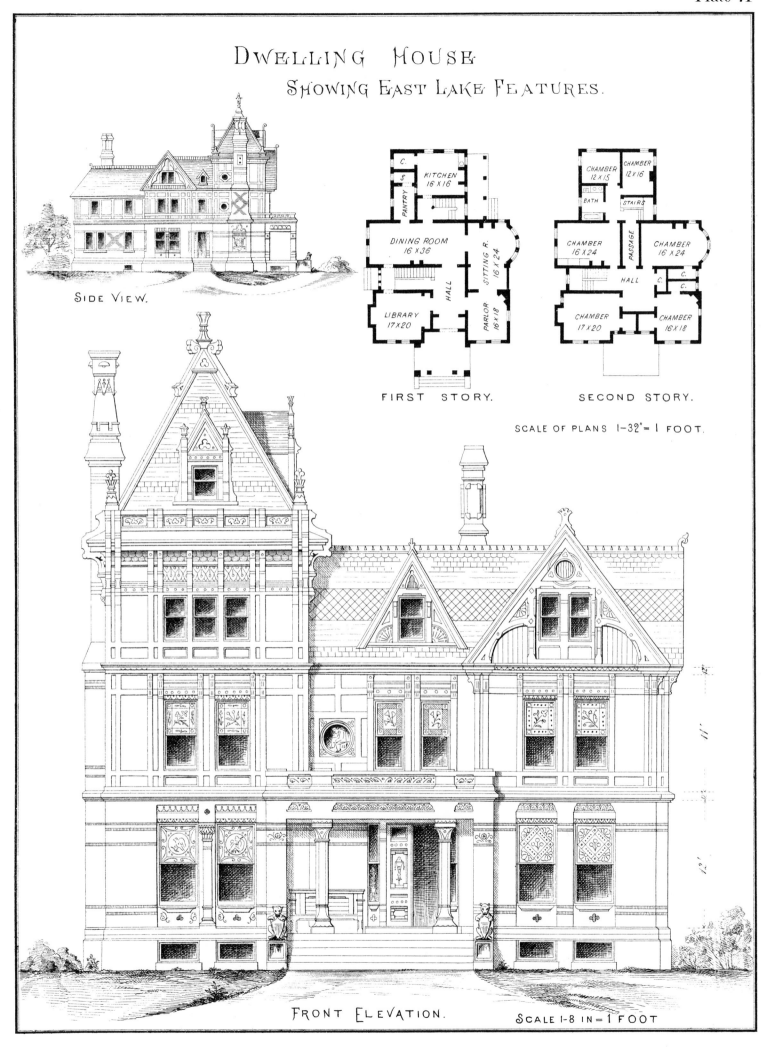

DWELLING HOUSE
SHOWING EAST LAKE FEATURES.

SIDE VIEW.

C.
S
PANTRY
KITCHEN
16 X 16

DINING ROOM
16 X 36

HALL

SITTING R.
16 X 24

PARLOR
16 X 18

LIBRARY
17 X 20

FIRST STORY.

CHAMBER
12 X 15
CHAMBER
12 X 16

BATH
STAIRS

CHAMBER
16 X 24
PASSAGE
CHAMBER
16 X 24

HALL
C.
C.
C.

CHAMBER
17 X 20
CHAMBER
16 X 18

SECOND STORY.

SCALE OF PLANS 1-32" = 1 FOOT.

FRONT ELEVATION.

SCALE 1-8 IN = 1 FOOT

Plate 72

Ventilators.

FIG. 1

FIG. 2

SCALE OF ELEVATIONS $\frac{1}{4}$ IN.=1 FT.
" " DETAILS $\frac{3}{4}$ IN.=1 FT.

N — S

FIG. 3

FIG. 4

Plate 73

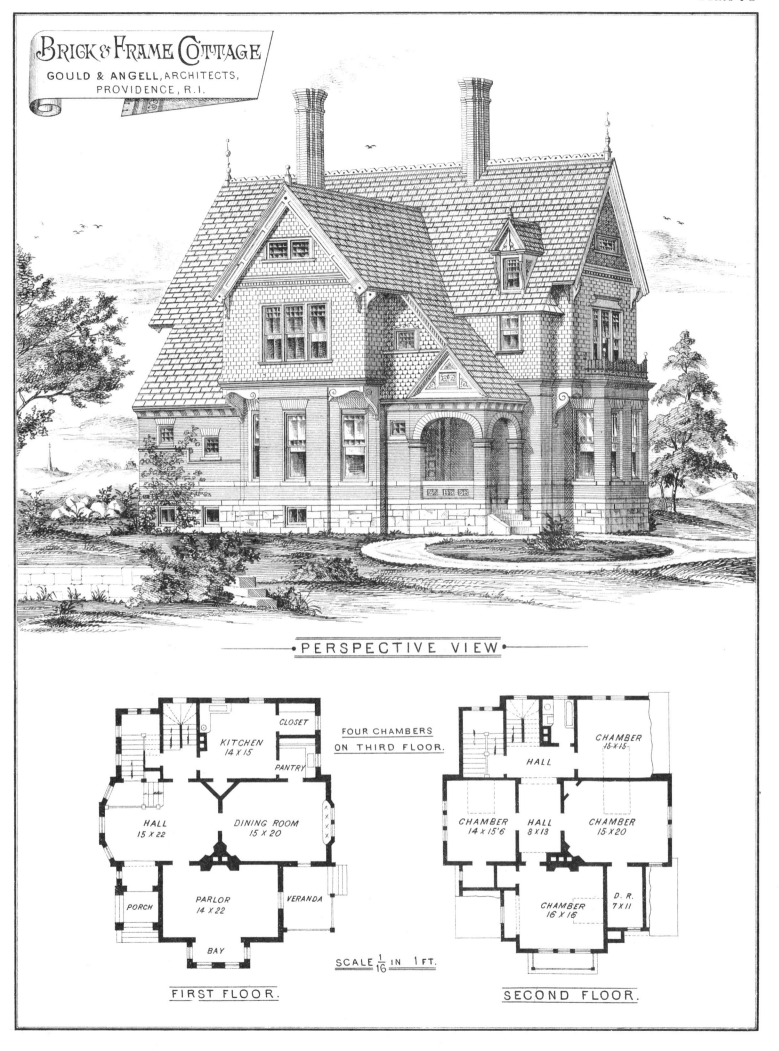

BRICK & FRAME COTTAGE
GOULD & ANGELL, ARCHITECTS,
PROVIDENCE, R.I.

• PERSPECTIVE VIEW •

CLOSET

KITCHEN
14 X 15

PANTRY

FOUR CHAMBERS
ON THIRD FLOOR.

CHAMBER
15 X 15

HALL

HALL
15 X 22

DINING ROOM
15 X 20

CHAMBER
14 X 15'6

HALL
8 X 13

CHAMBER
15 X 20

PORCH

PARLOR
14 X 22

VERANDA

CHAMBER
16 X 16

D. R.
7 X 11

BAY

SCALE 1/16 IN 1 FT.

FIRST FLOOR.

SECOND FLOOR.

Plate 74

ELEVATIONS OF DESIGN PLATE Nº 73.

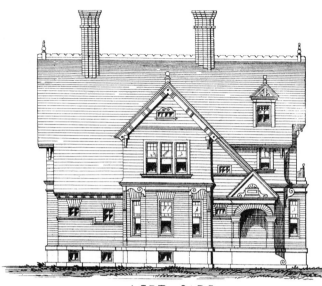

LEFT SIDE.

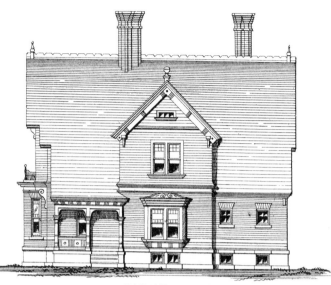

RIGHT SIDE.

Scale 1/16 in = 1 foot.

FRONT

Scale 1/8 in = 1 foot.

Plate 75

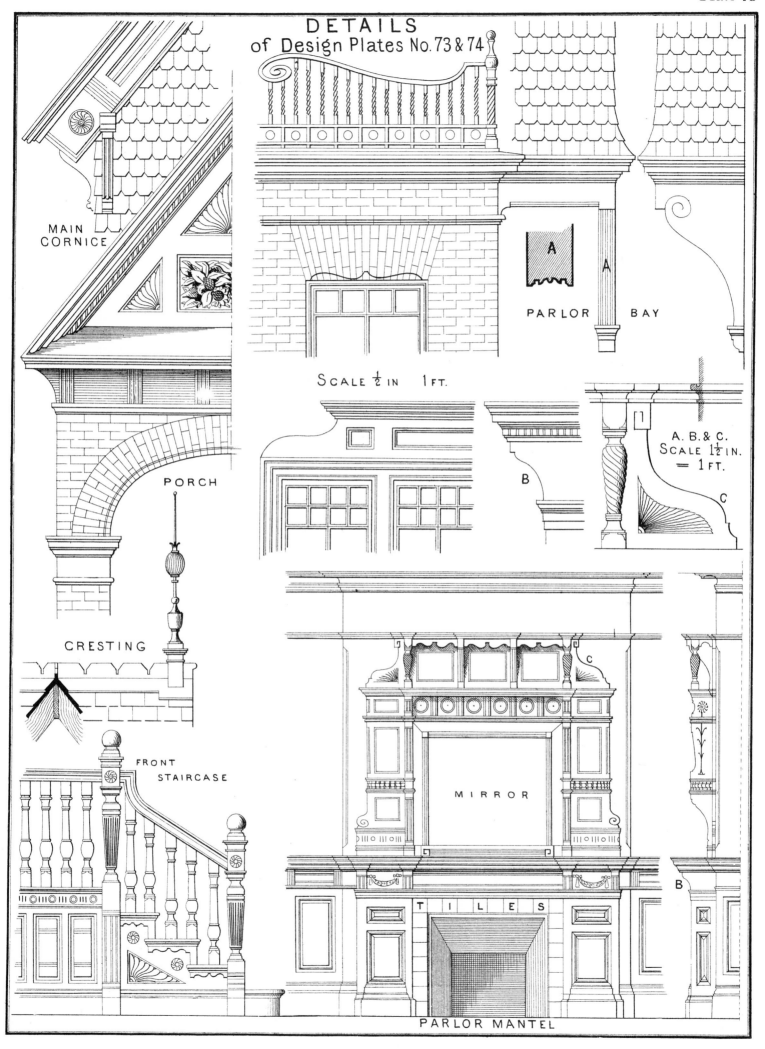

DETAILS
of Design Plates No. 73 & 74

MAIN CORNICE

PARLOR BAY

PORCH

SCALE ½ IN 1 FT.

A. B. & C.
SCALE 1½ IN.
= 1 FT.

B

C

CRESTING

FRONT STAIRCASE

MIRROR

TILES

B

PARLOR MANTEL

Plate 76

Dwelling in the Elizabethan Style.

Front Elevation.

Side Elevation.

Scale ³⁄₃₂" = 1 foot

First Story.

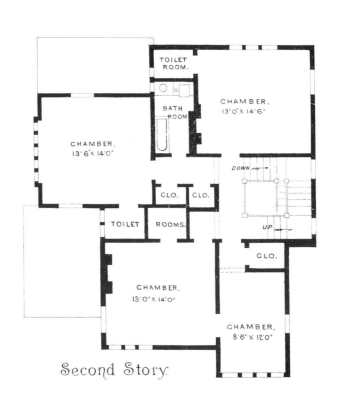

Second Story.

Plate 77

ELEVATIONS & SECTIONS OF COUNTER AND SCREEN.

SECTION.

FITTINGS

FOR

BANKING

OR

INSURANCE OFFICE

SCALE $\frac{1}{2}$ INCH

TO 1 FOOT.

SECTION.

ELEVATION OF A PARTITION.

ELEVATION OF BALUSTERS RAIL &C.

SIDE   DESK   FRONT

Plate 78

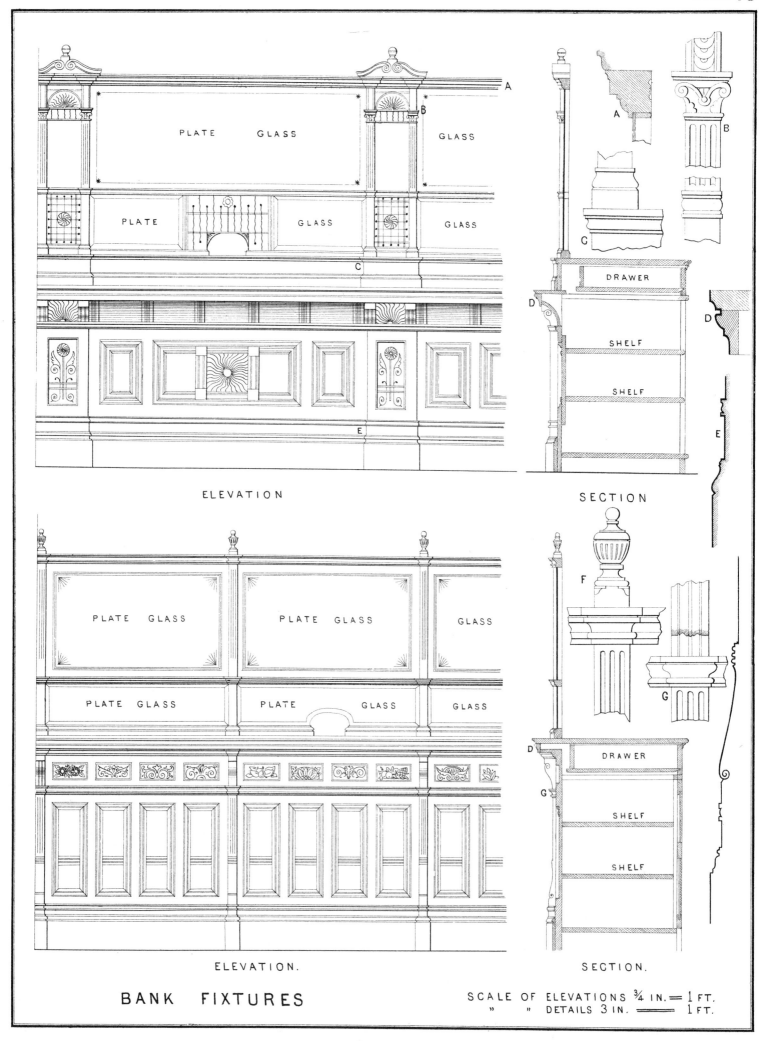

ELEVATION

SECTION

ELEVATION.

SECTION.

BANK FIXTURES

SCALE OF ELEVATIONS ¾ IN. = 1 FT.
"   "   DETAILS 3 IN. ——— 1 FT.

Plate 79

DESIGNED FOR A DINING ROOM
FINISHED IN CHERRY.

CIRCULAR VENTILATING REGISTERS IN CUT BRASS.
SCALE 1/3 FULL SIZE.

VENTILATING REGISTERS.
SCALE 1/4 FULL SIZE.

CUT BRASS VENTILATING REGISTER IN SPANDRIL.

SCALE 1/3 FULL SIZE

VENTILATING REGISTERS IN SPANDRILS

SCALE 1/3 FULL SIZE.

J. P. Putnam, Architect, Boston.

Plate 80

CHIMNEY TOPS.

SCALE ½ IN = 1 FT.

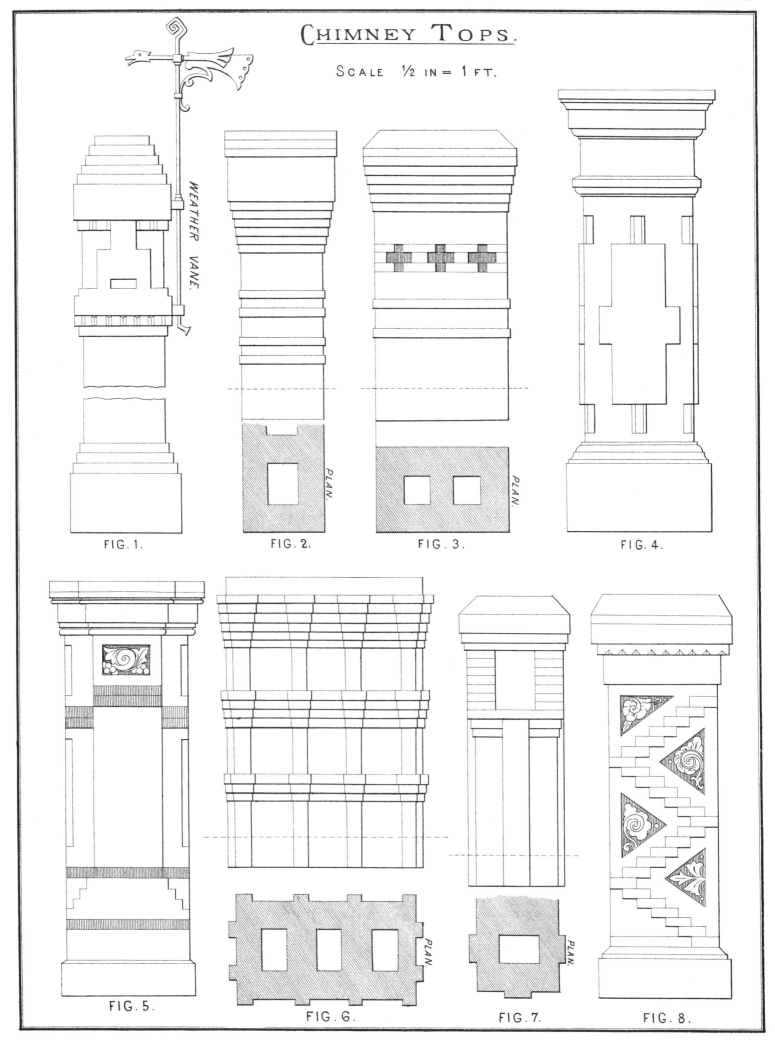

WEATHER VANE.

FIG. 1.

PLAN.

FIG. 2.

PLAN.

FIG. 3.

FIG. 4.

FIG. 5.

PLAN.

FIG. 6.

PLAN.

FIG. 7.

FIG. 8.